CAMBRIDGE LIBRARY COLLECTION

Books of enduring scholarly value

Travel and Exploration

The history of travel writing dates back to the Bible, Caesar, the Vikings and the Crusaders, and its many themes include war, trade, science and recreation. Explorers from Columbus to Cook charted lands not previously visited by Western travellers, and were followed by merchants, missionaries, and colonists, who wrote accounts of their experiences. The development of steam power in the nineteenth century provided opportunities for increasing numbers of 'ordinary' people to travel further, more economically, and more safely, and resulted in great enthusiasm for travel writing among the reading public. Works included in this series range from first-hand descriptions of previously unrecorded places, to literary accounts of the strange habits of foreigners, to examples of the burgeoning numbers of guidebooks produced to satisfy the needs of a new kind of traveller - the tourist.

Two Trips to Gorilla Land and the Cataracts of the Congo

Sir Richard Burton (1821–90) is well known for his colourful career, recorded in numerous books and articles, as a diplomat, explorer and ethnographer. In 1861 he was appointed consul to Fernando Po (now Bioko) in Equatorial Guinea, remaining there for four years until he was transferred to Brazil. These volumes collate the expeditions and ethnographic observations made during his time there. In his preface, Burton writes that the 'plain truth' about the African has not been told in Britain, declaring that English occupation of West Africa has proved 'a remarkable failure'. First published in 1876, Volume 1 records Burton's landing at the Gaboon River and includes geographical details, information about local tribes, and reports of journeys to Sanga Tanga and up the Gaboon River to its source. Burton also writes about a 'specimen day' with the reputed Fán cannibals and includes a chapter on gorillas.

Cambridge University Press has long been a pioneer in the reissuing of out-of-print titles from its own backlist, producing digital reprints of books that are still sought after by scholars and students but could not be reprinted economically using traditional technology. The Cambridge Library Collection extends this activity to a wider range of books which are still of importance to researchers and professionals, either for the source material they contain, or as landmarks in the history of their academic discipline.

Drawing from the world-renowned collections in the Cambridge University Library, and guided by the advice of experts in each subject area, Cambridge University Press is using state-of-the-art scanning machines in its own Printing House to capture the content of each book selected for inclusion. The files are processed to give a consistently clear, crisp image, and the books finished to the high quality standard for which the Press is recognised around the world. The latest print-on-demand technology ensures that the books will remain available indefinitely, and that orders for single or multiple copies can quickly be supplied.

The Cambridge Library Collection will bring back to life books of enduring scholarly value (including out-of-copyright works originally issued by other publishers) across a wide range of disciplines in the humanities and social sciences and in science and technology.

Two Trips to Gorilla Land and the Cataracts of the Congo

VOLUME 1

RICHARD FRANCIS BURTON

CAMBRIDGE UNIVERSITY PRESS

Cambridge, New York, Melbourne, Madrid, Cape Town,
Singapore, São Paolo, Delhi, Tokyo, Mexico City

Published in the United States of America by Cambridge University Press, New York

www.cambridge.org
Information on this title: www.cambridge.org/9781108031349

This edition first published 1876
This digitally printed version 2011

ISBN 978-1-108-03134-9 Paperback

TWO TRIPS TO GORILLA LAND

AND THE CATARACTS OF

THE CONGO.

" Quisquis amat Congi fines peragrare nigrantes,
Africæ et Æthiopum cernere regna, domus,
* * * * * * *
Perlegat hunc librum."
FRA ANGELUS DE MAP. PICCARDUS.

" Timbuctoo travels, voyages to the poles,
Are ways to benefit mankind as true
Perhaps as shooting them at Waterloo."—DON JUAN.

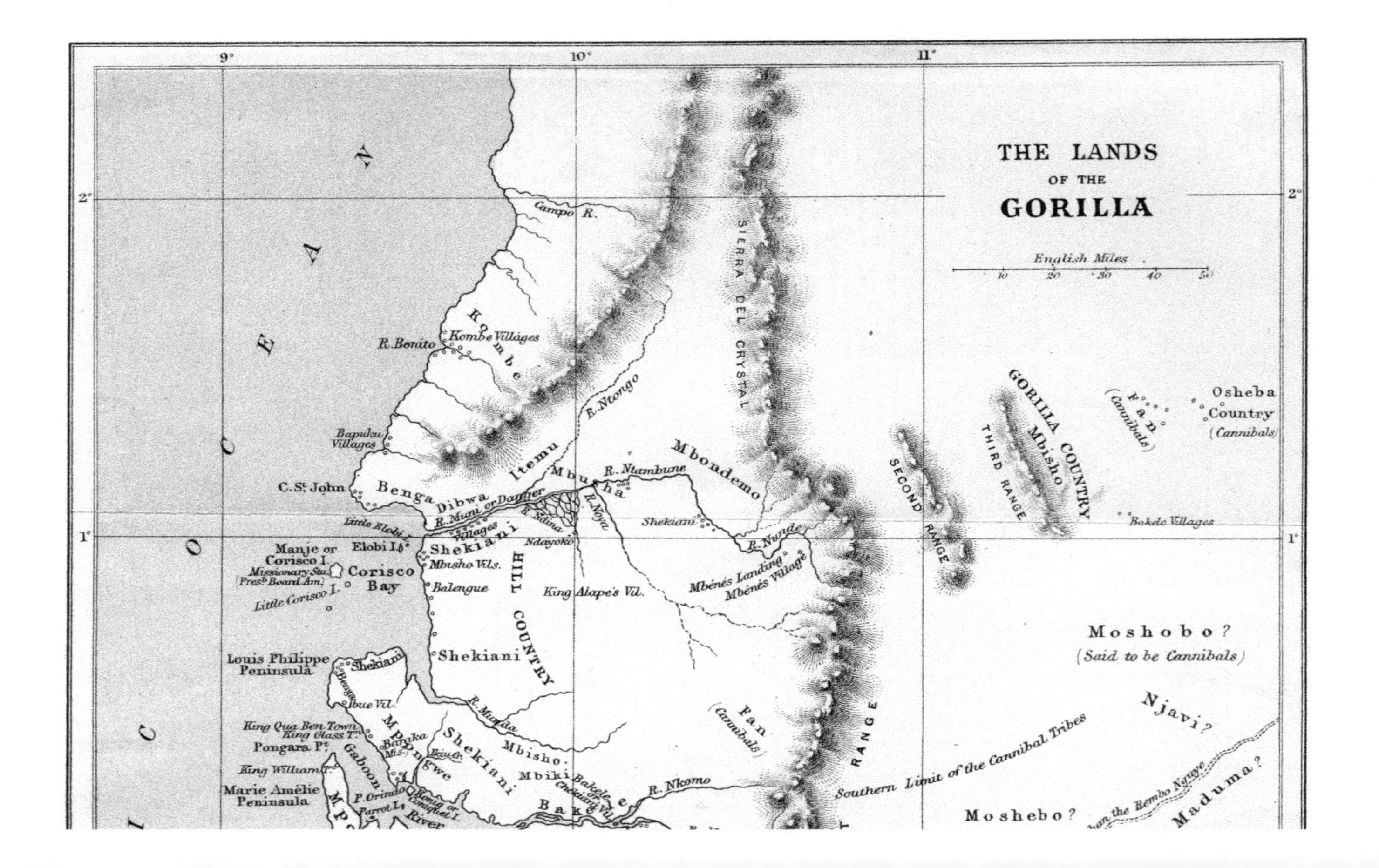
THE LANDS
OF THE
GORILLA
English Miles
10 20 30 40 50
9°
10°
11°
2°
1°
OCEAN
Campo R.
SIERRA DEL CRYSTAL
Kombe
Kombe Villages
R. Benito
Bapuku Villages
R. Ntongo
Itemu
C. St. John
Benga
Dibwa
R. Muni or Danger
Mbusha
R. Ntambune
Mbondemo
R. Ndina
R. Noya
Shekiani
R. Nunde
Little Elobi I.
Elobi Id.
Villages
Shekiani
Ndayoko
Manje or Corisco I.
Missionary Stn. (Presb. Board Am.)
Corisco Bay
Little Corisco I.
Mbusho Vls.
Balengue
HILL COUNTRY
King Alape's Vl.
Mbénés Landing
Mbénés Village
Louis Philippe Peninsula
Shekiani
Benga
Ibue Vl.
R. Munda
King Qua Ben Town
King Glass Tn.
Pongara Pt.
King William T.
Gaboon
Mpongwe
Baraka Mis.
Mbisho
Shekiani
Mbiki
Bakele or Chekiani Vl.
R. Nkomo
Marie Amélie Peninsula
P. Orindo
Parrot I.
Konig or Coniquet I.
River
Fan (Cannibals)
Southern Limit of the Cannibal Tribes
RANGE
SECOND RANGE
GORILLA COUNTRY
Mbisho
THIRD RANGE
Fan (Cannibals)
Osheba Country (Cannibals)
Bakele Villages
Moshobo ?
(Said to be Cannibals)
Njavi ?
Moshebo ?
Maduma ?
the Rembo Nguye

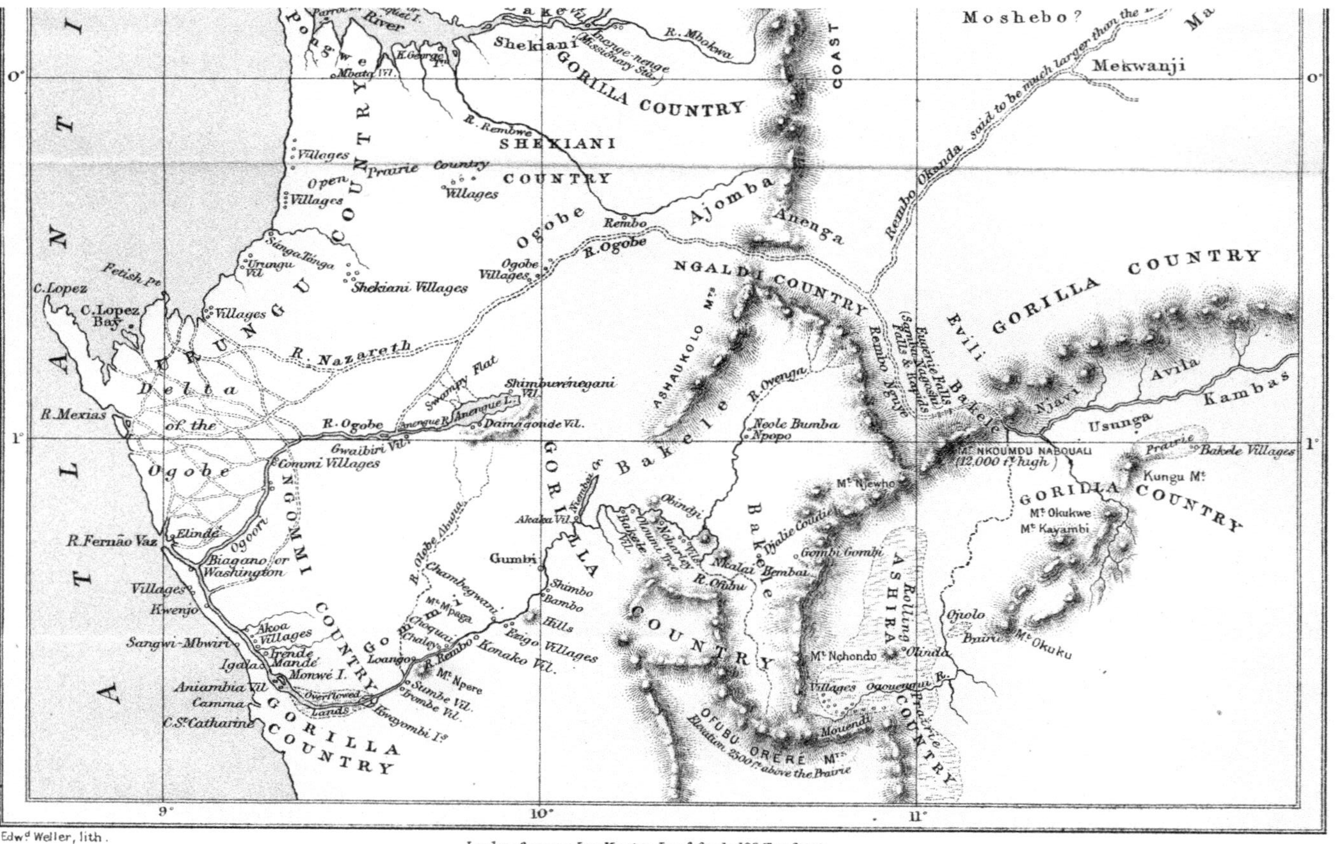
Moshebo?
Mekwanji
Rembo Okanda said to be much larger than the
COAST
Shekiani
Inange-nenge Missionary Sta.
R. Mbokwa
GORILLA COUNTRY
R. Rembwe
SHEKIANI
COUNTRY
Prairie Country
Villages
Open
Ajomba
Anenga
Rembo
Ogobe
R. Ogobe
Ogobe Villages
NGALDI COUNTRY
Shekiani Villages
C. Lopez
C. Lopez Bay
Fetish Pt.
R. Nazareth
Delta of the Ogobe
R. Mexias
Swampy Flat
Shimburénegani Vil.
R. Ogobe
Gwaibiri Vil.
Commi Villages
Damagonde Vil.
ASHAUKOLO Mts.
R. Owenga
Neole Bumba
Npopo
Rembo Nguye
Eugénie Falls (Samba Nagoshi) Falls & Rapids
Evili
Bakele
GORILLA COUNTRY
Njavi
Avila
Kambas
Usunga
Mt. NKOUMDU NABOUALI (12,000 ft. high)
Prairie
Bakele Villages
Kungu Mt.
GORILLA COUNTRY
Mt. Okukwe
Mt. Kayambi
Mt. Njewho
Bakele
Obindji
Ncharley
Oloumi Tree
Bakele Vil.
Akaka Vil.
GORILLA
Gumbi
Shimbo
Bambo
Hills
Ezigo Villages
Konako Vil.
R. Ofubu
Nkalai
Bembai
Gombi Gombi
Djalie Coudie
ASHIRA
Rolling
COUNTRY
Mt. Nchondo
Olinda
Ogouenui R.
Prairie
Villages
Ojolo
Bairu
Mt. Okuku
OFUBU ORERE Mts.
Mouendi
Elevation 2500 ft. above the Prairie
R. Fernão Vaz
Elinde
Ogoori
Biagano or Washington
NGOMMI COUNTRY
R. Olobe Alouna
Chambegwani
Mt. Mpaga
Choquai
Chaley
Loango
R. Rembo
Mt. Npere
Sumbe Vil.
Dombe Vil.
Hwayombi Is.
Villages
Kwenjo
Akoa Villages
Sangwi-Mbwiri
Igala
Irende
Mande
Monwé I.
Aniambia Vil.
Camma
C. St. Catharine
Overflowed Lands
GORILLA COUNTRY
ATLANTIC
0°
1°
9°
10°
11°
Edwd. Weller, lith.
London: Sampson Low, Marston, Low & Searle, 188 Fleet Street.

TWO TRIPS TO

GORILLA LAND

AND THE CATARACTS

OF THE CONGO.

BY

RICHARD F. BURTON.

IN TWO VOLUMES.

VOL. I.

LONDON:

SAMPSON LOW, MARSTON, LOW, AND SEARLE,

CROWN BUILDINGS, FLEET STREET.

1876.

CHISWICK PRESS:—PRINTED BY WHITTINGHAM AND WILKINS,
TOOKS COURT, CHANCERY LANE.

TRIESTE, *Jan.* 31, 1875.

MY DEAR SIR GEORGE,

OUR paths in life have been separated by a long interval. Whilst inclination led you to explore and to survey the wild wastes of the North, the Arctic shores and the Polar seas, with all their hardships and horrors; my lot was cast in the torrid regions of Sind and Arabia; in the luxuriant deserts of Africa, and in the gorgeous tropical forests of the Brazil. But the true traveller can always appreciate the record of another's experience, and perhaps the force of contrast makes him most enjoy the adventures differing the most from his own. To whom, then, more appropriately than to yourself, a discoverer of no ordinary note, a recorder of explorations, and, finally, an earnest labourer in the cause of geography, can I inscribe this plain, unvarnished tale of a soldier-traveller? Kindly accept the trifle as a token of the warmest esteem, an earnest of my thankfulness for the interest ever shown by you in forwarding my plans and projects of adventure; and, in the heartfelt hope that Allah may prolong your days, permit me to subscribe myself,

Your sincere admirer and grateful friend,

RICHARD F. BURTON.

Admiral Sir George Back, D.C.L., F.R.S.,
Vice-Pres. R.G.S., &c.

PREFACE.

HE notes which form the ground-work of these volumes have long been kept in the obscurity of manuscript: my studies of South America, of Syria and Palestine, of Iceland, and of Istria, left me scant time for the labour of preparation. Leisure and opportunity have now offered themselves, and I avail myself of them in the hope that the publication will be found useful to more than one class of readers. The many who take an interest in the life of barbarous peoples may not be displeased to hear more about the Fá*n*; and the few who would try a fall with Mister Gorilla can learn from me how to equip themselves, whence to set out and whither to go for the best chance. Travelling with M. Paul B. du Chaillu's "First Expedition" in my hand, I jealously looked into every statement, and his numerous friends will be pleased to see how many of his assertions are confirmed by my experience.

The second part is devoted to the Nzadi or

lower Congo River, from the mouth to the Yellala or main rapids, the gate by which the mighty stream, emerging from the plateau of Inner Africa, goes to its long home, the Atlantic. Some time must elapse before the second expedition, which left Ambriz early in 1873, under Lieutenant Grandy, R. N., can submit its labours to the public: meanwhile these pages will, I trust, form a suitable introduction to the gallant explorer's travel in the interior. It would be preposterous to publish descriptions of any European country from information gathered ten years ago. But Africa moves slowly, and thus we see that the results of an Abyssinian journey (M. Antoine d'Abbadie's "Géodésie d'Ethiopie," which took place about 1845, are not considered obsolete in 1873.

After a languid conviction during the last half century of owning some ground upon the West Coast of Africa, England has been rudely aroused by a little war which will have large consequences. The causes that led to the "Ashantee Campaign," a negro copy of the negroid Abyssinian, may be broadly laid down as general incuriousness, local mismanagement, and the operation of unprincipled journalism.

It is not a little amusing to hear the complaints of the public that plain truth about the African has not been told. I could cite more than one name that has done so. But what was the result?

We were all soundly abused by the negrophile; the multitude cared little about reading "unpopular opinions;" and then, when the fulness of time came, it turned upon us, and rent us, and asked why we had not spoken freely concerning Ashanti and Fanti, and all the herd. My "Wanderings in West Africa" is a case in point: so little has it been read, that a President of the Royal Geographical Society (African section of the Society of Arts Journal, Feb. 6, 1874) could state, "If Fantees are cowardly and lazy, Krumen are brave;" the latter being the most notorious poltroons on the West African seaboard.

The hostilities on the Gold Coast might have been averted with honour to ourselves at any time between 1863 and 1870, by a Colonial Office mission and a couple of thousand pounds. I need hardly say what has been the case now. The first steps were taken with needless disasters, and the effect has been far different from what we intended or what was advisable. For a score of years we (travellers) have been advising the English statesman not to despise the cunning of barbarous tribes, never to attempt finessing with Asiatic or African; to treat these races with perfect sincerity and truthfulness. I have insisted, and it is now seen with what reason, that every attempt at deception, at asserting the "thing which is not," will presently meet with the reward it deserves. I can only regret that my counsels have not made themselves heard.

Yet this ignoble war between barbarous tribes whom it has long been the fashion to pet, this poor scuffle between the breechloader and the Birmingham trade musket, may yet in one sense do good. It must perforce draw public attention to the West Coast of Africa, and raise the question, "What shall we do with it?" My humble opinion, expressed early in 1865 to the Right Honourable Mr. Adderley, has ever been this. If we are determined not to follow the example of the French, the Dutch, the Portuguese, and the Spaniards, and not to use the country as a convict station, resolving to consume, as it were, our crime at home, we should also resolve to retain only a few ports and forts, without territory, at points commanding commerce, after the fashion of the Lusitanians in the old heroic days. The export slave-trade is now dead and buried; the want of demand must prevent its revival; and free emigration has yet to be created. As Mr. Bright rightly teaches, strong places and garrisons are not necessary to foster trade and to promote the success of missions. The best proof on the West African Coast is to be found in the so-called Oil Rivers, where we have never held a mile of ground, and where our commerce prospers most. The great "Tribune" will forgive my agreeing in opinion with him when he finds that we differ upon one most important point. It is the merchant, not the garrison, that causes African wars. If the home authorities would avoid a campaign, let them commit their difficulty to a soldier, not to a civilian.

The chronic discontent of the so-called "civilized" African, the contempt of the rulers if not of the rule, and the bitter hatred between the three races, white, black, and black-white, fomented by many an unprincipled print, which fills its pocket with coin of cant and Christian charity, will end in even greater scandals than the last disreputable war. If the *damnosa licentia* be not suppressed—and where are the strong hands to suppress it?—we may expect to see the scenes of Jamaica revived with improvements at Sierra Leone. However unwilling I am to cut off any part of our great and extended empire, to renew anywhere, even in Africa, the process of dismemberment—the policy which cast off Corfu—it is evident to me that English occupation of the West African Coast has but slightly forwarded the cause of humanity, and that upon the whole it has proved a remarkable failure.

We can be wise in time.

RICHARD F. BURTON.

P.S.—Since these pages were written, a name

which frequently occurs in them has become a memory to his friends—I allude to W. Winwood Reade, and I deplore his loss. The highest type of Englishman, brave and fearless as he was gentle and loving, his short life of thirty-seven years shows how much may be done by the honest, thorough worker. He had emphatically the courage of his opinions, and he towered a cubit above the crowd by telling not only the truth, as most of us do, but the whole truth, which so few can afford to do. His personal courage in battle during the Ashanti campaign, where the author of "Savage Africa" became correspondent of the "Times," is a matter of history. His noble candour in publishing the "Martyrdom of Man" is an example and a model to us who survive him. And he died calmly and courageously as he lived, died in harness, died as he had resolved to die, like the good and gallant gentleman of ancient lineage that he was.

CONTENTS OF VOL. I.

CHAPTER VIII.

CHAPTER IX.

CHAPTER X.

CHAPTER. XI.

CHAPTER XII.

PART I.

THE GABOON RIVER AND GORILLA LAND.

"It was my hint to speak, such was my process;
And of the cannibals that each other eat,
The anthropophagi, and men whose heads
Do grow beneath their shoulders."—OTHELLO.

PART I.

TRIP TO GORILLA LAND.

CHAPTER I.

LANDING AT THE RIO GABÃO (GABOON RIVER).—LE PLATEAU, THE FRENCH COLONY.

REMEMBER with lively pleasure my first glance at the classic stream of the "Portingal Captains" and the "Zeeland interlopers." The ten-mile breadth of the noble Gaboon estuary somewhat dwarfed the features of either shore as we rattled past Cape Santa Clara, a venerable name, "'verted" to Joinville. The bold northern head, though not "very high land," makes some display, because we see it in a better light; and its environs are set off by a line of scattered villages. The *vis-à-vis* of Louis Philippe Peninsula on the starboard bow (Zuidhoeck), "Sandy Point" or

Sandhoeck, by the natives called Pongára, and by the French Péninsule de Marie-Amélie, shows a mere fringe of dark bristle, which is tree, based upon a broad red-yellow streak, which is land. As we pass through the slightly overhung mouth, we can hardly complain with a late traveller of the Gaboon's "sluggish waters;" during the ebb they run like a mild mill-race, and when the current, setting to the north-west, meets a strong sea-breeze from the west, there is a criss-cross, a tide-rip, contemptible enough to a cruizer, but quite capable of filling cock-boats. And, nearing the end of our voyage, we rejoice to see that the dull down-pourings and the sharp storms of Fernando Po have apparently not yet migrated so far south. Dancing blue wavelets, under the soft azure sky, plash and cream upon the pure clean sand that projects here and there black lines of porous iron-stone waiting to become piers; and the water-line is backed by swelling ridges, here open and green-grassed, there spotted with islets of close and shady trees. Mangrove, that horror of the African voyager, shines by its absence; and the soil is not mud, but humus based on gravels or on ruddy clays, stiff and retentive. The formation, in fact, is everywhere that of Eyo or Yoruba, the goodly region lying west of the lower Niger, and its fertility must result from the abundant water-supply of the equatorial belt.

The charts are fearful to look upon. The embouchure, well known to old traders, has been scientifically surveyed in our day by Lieutenant Alph. Fleuriot de Langle, of La Malouine (1845), and the chart was corrected from a survey ordered by Capitaine Bouët-Willaümez (1849); in the latter year it was again revised by M. Charles

LE PLATEAU, FRENCH CAPITAL OF THE GABOON.

Floix, of the French navy, and, with additions by the officers of Her Britannic Majesty's service, it becomes our No. 1877. The surface is a labyrinth of banks, rocks, and shoals, "Ely," Nisus," "Alligator," and "Caraibe." In such surroundings as these, when the water shallows apace, the pilot must not be despised.

Her Majesty's steam-ship "Griffon," Commander Perry, found herself, at 2 P.M. on Monday, March,

17, 1862, in a snug berth opposite Le Plateau, as the capital of the French colony is called, and amongst the shipping of its chief port, Aumale Road. The river at this neck is about five miles broad, and the scene was characteristically French. Hardly a merchant vessel lay there. We had no less than four naval consorts "La Caravane," guard-ship, store-ship, and hospital-hulk; a fine transport, "La Riège," bound for Goree; "La Recherche," a wretched old sailing corvette which plies to Assini and Grand Basam on the Gold Coast; and, lastly, "La Junon," chef de division Baron Didelot, then one of the finest frigates in the French navy, armed with fifty rifled sixty-eight pounders. It is curious that, whilst our neighbours build such splendid craft, and look so neat and natty in naval uniform, they pay so little regard to the order and cleanliness of their floating homes.

After visiting every English colony on the West Coast of Africa, I resolved curiously to examine my first specimen of our rivals, the "principal centre of trade in western equatorial Africa." The earliest visit—in uniform, of course—was to Baron Didelot, whose official title is "Commandant Supérieur des Établissements de la Côte d'Or et du Gabon;" the following was to M. H. S. L'Aulnois, "Lieutenant de Vaisseau et Commandant Particulier du Comptoir de Gabon." These gentlemen have neat bungalows and gardens; they may spend their days ashore, but they are very careful to sleep on board. All the official whites appear to have a morbid horror of the climate; when attacked by fever, they "cave in" at once, and recovery can hardly be expected. This year also, owing to scanty rains, sickness has been rife, and many cases which began with normal mildness have ended suddenly and fatally. Besides fear of fever, they are victims to *ennui* and *nostalgia;* and, expecting the Comptoir to pay large profits, they are greatly disappointed by the reverse being the case.

But how can they look for it to be otherwise? The modern French appear fit to manage only garrisons and military posts. They *will* make everything official, and they will *not* remember the protest against governing too much, offered by the burgesses of Paris to Louis le Grand. They are *always* on duty; they are *never* out of uniform, mentally and metaphorically, as well as bodily and literally. Nothing is done without delay, even in the matter of signing a ship's papers. A long *procès-verbal* takes the place of our summary punishment, and the *gros canon* is dragged into use on every occasion, even to enforce the payment of native debts.

In the Gaboon, also, there is a complication of national jealousy, suggesting the mastiff and the poodle. A perpetual war rages about flags.

English craft may carry their colours as far up stream as Coniquet Island; beyond this point they must either hoist a French ensign, or sail without bunting—should the commodore permit. Otherwise they will be detained by the commander of the hulk "l'Oise," stationed at Anenge-nenge, some thirty-eight to forty miles above Le Plateau. Lately a Captain Gordon, employed by Mr. Francis Wookey of Taunton, was ordered to pull down his flag: those who know the "mariner of England" will appreciate his feelings on the occasion. Small vessels belonging to foreigners, and employed in cabotage, must not sail with their own papers, and even a change of name is effected under difficulties. About a week before my arrival a certain pan-Teutonic Hamburgher, Herr B——, amused himself, after a copious breakfast, with hoisting and saluting the Union Jack, in honour of a distinguished guest, Major L——. A report was at once spread that the tricolor had been hauled down "with extreme indignity;" and the Commodore took the trouble to reprimand the white, and to imprison "Tom Case," the black in whose town the outrage had been allowed.

This by way of parenthesis. My next step was to request the pleasure of a visit from Messrs. Hogg and Kirkwood, who were in charge of the English factories at Glass Town and Olomi; they came down stream at once, and kindly acted as ciceroni around Le Plateau. The landing is good; a reef has been converted into a jetty and little breakwater; behind this segment of a circle we disembarked without any danger of being washed out of the boat, as at S'a Leone, Cape Coast Castle, and Accra. Unfortunately just above this pier there is a Dutch-like *jardin d'été*—beds of dirty weeds bordering a foul and stagnant swamp, while below the settlement appears a huge coal-shed: the expensive mineral is always dangerous when exposed in the tropics, and some thirty per cent. would be saved by sending out a hulk. The next point is the Hotel and Restaurant Fischer—pronounced Fi-cherre, belonging to an energetic German-Swiss widow, who during six years' exile had amassed some 65,000 francs. In an evil hour she sent a thieving servant before the "commissaire de police;" the negress escaped punishment, but the verandah with its appurtenances caught fire, and everything, even the unpacked billiard-table, was burnt to ashes. Still, Madame the Brave never lost heart. She applied herself valiantly as a white ant to repairing her broken home, and, wonderful to relate in this land of no labour, ruled by the maxim "*festina lente*," all had been restored within six months. We shall dine at her *table d'hôte*.

Our guide led up and along the river bank, where there is almost a kilometre of road facing six or seven kilometres of nature's highway—the stream. The swampy jungle is not cleared off from about the Comptoir, and presently the perfume of the fat, rank weeds; and the wretched bridges, a few planks spanning black and fetid mud, drove us northwards or inland, towards the neat house and grounds of the "Commandant Particulier." The outside walls, built in grades with the porous, dark-red, laterite-like stone dredged from the river, are whitewashed with burnt coralline and look clean; whilst the house, one of the best in the place, is French, that is to say, pretty. Near it is a cluster of native huts, mostly with walls of corded bamboo, some dabbed with clay and lime, and all roofed with the ever shabby-looking palm-leaf; none are as neat as those of the "bushmen" in the interior, where they are regularly and carefully made like baskets or panniers. The people appeared friendly; the men touched their hats, and the women dropped unmistakably significant curtsies.

After admiring the picturesque bush and the natural avenues behind Le Plateau, we diverged towards the local Père-la-Chaise. The new cemetery, surrounded by a tall stone wall and approached by a large locked gate, contains only four tombs; the old burial ground opposite is unwalled, open, and painfully crowded; the trees have run wild, the crosses cumber the ground, the gravestones are tilted up and down; in fact the foul Golgotha of Santos, São Paulo, the Brazil, is not more ragged, shabby, and neglected. We were shown the last resting-place of M. du Chaillu père, agent to Messrs. Oppenheim, the old Parisian house: he died here in 1856.

Resuming our way parallel with, but distant from the river, we passed a bran-new military store-house, bright with whitewash. Outside the compound lay the lines of the "Zouaves," some forty negroes whom Goree has supplied to the Gaboon; they were accompanied by a number of intelligent mechanics, who loudly complained of having been kidnapped, coolie-fashion. We then debouched upon Fort Aumale; from the anchorage it appears a whitewashed square, whose feet are dipped in bright green vegetation, and its head wears a dingy brown roof-thatch. A nearer view shows a pair of semi-detached houses, built upon arches, and separated by a thoroughfare; the cleaner of the two is a hospital; the dingier, which is decorated with the brown-green stains, the normal complexion of tropical masonry, lodges the station Commandant and the medical officers. Fronting the former and by the side of an avenue that runs towards the sea is an unfinished magazine of stone, and to the right, as you front the sun, lies the garden of the "Commandant du Comptoir," choked with tropical weeds. Altogether there is a scattered look about the metropolis of the "Gabon," which numbers one foot of house to a thousand of "compound."

Suddenly a bonnet like a pair of white gulls' wings and a blue serge gown fled from us, despite the weight of years, like a young gazelle; the wearer was a sister of charity, one of five *bonnes sœurs.* Their bungalow is roomy and comfortable, near a little chapel and a largish school, whence issue towards sunset the well-known sounds of the Angelus. At some distance down stream and on the right or northern bank lies a convent, and a house superintended by the original establisher of the mission in 1844, the bishop, Mgr. Bessieux, who died in 1872, aged 70. There are extensive plantations, but the people are too lazy to take example from them.

Before we hear the loud cry *à table*, we may shortly describe the civilized career of the Gaboon. In 1842, when French and English rivalry, burning hot on both sides of the Channel, extended deep into the tropics and spurned the equator, and when every naval officer, high and low, went mad about concluding treaties and conquering territory on paper, France was persuaded to set up a naval station in Gorilla-land. The northern and the southern shore each had a king, whose consent, after a careless fashion, was considered decorous. His Majesty of the North was old King

Glass[1] and his chief "tradesman," that is, his premier, was the late Toko, a shrewd and far-seeing statesman. His Majesty of the South was Rapwensembo, known to the English as King William, to the French as Roi Denis.

Matters being in this state, M. le Comte Bouët-Willaumez, then Capitaine de Vaisseau and Governor of Senegal, resolved, *coûte que coûte*, to have his fortified Comptoir. Evidently the northern shore was preferable; it was more populous and more healthy, facing the fresh southerly winds. During the preliminary negotiations Toko, partial to the English, whose language he spoke fluently, and with whom the Glass family had ever been friendly, thwarted the design with all his might, and, despite threats and bribes, honestly kept up his opposition to the last. Roi Denis, on the other hand, who had been decorated with the Légion d'Honneur for saving certain shipwrecked sailors, who knew French well, and who hoped to be made king of the whole country, favoured to the utmost Gallic views, taking especial care, however, to place the broad river between himself and his white friends. M. de Moleon, Capitaine de Frégate, and commanding the brig "Le Zèbre," occupied the place, Mr.

---

[1] Paul B. du Chaillu, Chap. III. "Explorations and Adventures in Equatorial Africa." London: Murray, 1861.

Wilson ("Western Africa," p. 254) says by force of arms, but that is probably an exaggeration. To bring our history to an end, the sons of Japheth overcame the children of Ham, and, as the natives said, "Toko he muss love Frenchman, all but out of (*anglicè* 'in') his heart."

As in the streets of Paris, so in every French city at home and abroad,

"Verborum vetus interit ætas,"

and an old colonial chart often reads like a lesson in modern history. Here we still find under the Empire the Constitutional Monarchy of 1842-3. Mount Bouët leads to Fort "Aumale:" Point Joinville, at the north jaw of the river, faces Cap Montagniés: Parrot has become "Adelaide," and Coniquet "Orleans" Island. Indeed the love of Louis-Philippe's family has lingered in many a corner where one would least expect to meet it, and in 1869 I found "Port Saeed" a hot-bed of Orleanism.

The hotel verandah was crowded with the minor officials, the surgeons, and the clerks of the comptoir, drinking absinthe and colicky vermouth, smoking veritable "weeds," playing at dominoes, and contending who could talk longest and loudest.

---

[1] Rev. J. Leighton Wilson of the Presbyterian Mission, eighteen years in Africa, "Western Africa," &c. New York. Harpers, 1856.

At 7 P.M. the word was given to "fall to." The room was small and exceedingly close; the social board was big and very rickety. The *clientèle* rushed in like backwoodsmen on board a Mississippi floating-palace, stripped off their coats, tucked up their sleeves, and, knife in one hand and bread in the other, advanced gallantly to the fray. They began by quarrelling about carving; one made a sporting offer to *découper la soupe*, but he would go no farther; and Madame, as the head of the table, ended by asking my factotum, Selim Agha, to "have the kindness." The din, the heat, the flare of composition candles which gave 45 per cent. less of light than they ought, the blunders of the slaves, the objurgations of the hostess, and the spectacled face opposite me, were as much as I could bear, and a trifle more. No wonder that the resident English merchants avoid the *table-d'hôte*.

Provisions are dear and scarce at the Gaboon, where, as in other parts of West Africa, the negro will not part with his animals, unless paid at the rate of some twenty-two or twenty-three shillings for a lean goat or sheep. Yet the dinner is copious; the *employés* contribute their rations; and thus the table shows beef twice a week. Black cattle are imported from various parts of the coast, north and south; perhaps those of the Kru country stand the climate best; the Government yard is well stocked, and the polite Commodore readily allows our cruizers to buy bullocks. Madame also is not a "bird with a long bill;" the dinner, including *piquette,* alias *vin ordinaire,* coffee, and the *petit verre,* costs five francs to the stranger, and one franc less pays the *déjeuner à la fourchette*—most men here eat two dinners. The *soi-disant* Médoc (forty francs per dozen) is tolerable, and the cassis (thirty francs) is drinkable. I am talking in the present of things twelve years past. What a shadowy, ghostly *table d'hôte* it has now become to me!

After dinner appeared cigar and pipe, which were enjoyed in the verandah: I sat up late, admiring the intense brilliancy of the white and blue lightning, but auguring badly for the future,—natives will not hunt during the rains. A strong wind was blowing from the north-east, which, with the north-north-east, is here, as at Fernando Po and Camaronen, the stormy quarter. A "dry tornado," however, was the only result that night.

My trip to Gorilla-land was limited by the cruise upon which H.M. S.S. "Griffon" had been ordered, namely, to and from the South Coast with mail-bags. Many of those whom I had wished to see were absent; but Mr. Hogg set to work in the most business-like style. He borrowed a boat from the Rev. William Walker, of the Gaboon Mission, who kindly wrote that I should have something less cranky if I could wait awhile; he manned it with three of his own Krumen, and he collected the necessary stores and supplies of cloth, pipes and tobacco, rum, white wine, and absinthe for the natives.

My private stores cost some 200 francs. They consisted of candles, sugar, bread, cocoa, desiccated milk, and potatoes; Cognac and Médoc; ham, sausages, soups, and preserved meats, the latter French and, as usual, very good and very dear. The total expenditure for twelve days was 300 francs.

My indispensables were reduced to three loads, and I had four "pull-a-boys," one a Mpongwe, Mwáká *alias* Captain Merrick, a model sluggard; and Messrs. Smoke, Joe Williams, and Tom Whistle—Kru-men, called Kru-boys. This is not upon the principle, as some suppose, of the grey-headed post-boy and drummer-boy: all the Kraoh tribes end their names in bo, *e.g.* Worebo, from "wore," to capsize a canoe; Grebo, from the monkey "gre" or "gle;" and many others. Bo became "boy," even as Sipahi (Sepoy) became Sea-pie, and Sukhani (steersman) Sea-Coney.

Gaboon is French, with a purely English trade. Gambia is English, with a purely French trade; the latter is the result of many causes, but especially of the large neighbouring establishments at Goree, Saint Louis de Sénégal, and Saint Joseph de Galam. Exchanging the two was long held the soundest of policy. The French hoped by it to secure their darling object,—exclusive possession of the maritime regions, as well as the interior, leading to the gold mines of the Mandengas (Mandingas), and allowing overland connection with their Algerine colony. The English also seemed willing enough to "swop" an effete and dilapidated settlement, surrounded by more powerful rivals—a hot-bed of dysentery and yellow fever, a blot upon the fair face of earth, even African earth—for a new and fresh country, with a comparatively good climate, in which the thermometer ranges between 65° (Fahr.) and 90°, with a barometer as high as the heat allows; and where, being at home and unwatched, they could subject a lingering slave-trade to a regular British putting-down. But, when matters came to the point in 1870-71, the proposed bargain excited a storm of sentimental wrath which was as queer as unexpected. The French object to part with the Gaboon, as the Germans appear inclined to settle upon the Ogobe River. In England, cotton, civilization, and even Christianity were thrust forward by half-a-dozen merchants, and by a few venal colonial prints. The question assumed the angriest aspect; and, lastly, the Prussian-French war underwrote the negotiations with a *finis pro temp.* I hope to see them renewed; and I hope still more ardently to see the day when we shall either put our so-called "colonies" on the West Coast of Africa to their only proper use, convict stations, or when, if we are determined upon consuming our own crime at home, we shall make up our minds to restore them to the negro and the hyæna, their "old inhabitants."

At the time of my visit, the Gaboon River had four English traders; viz.

1. Messrs. Laughland and Co., provision-merchants, Fernando Po and Glasgow. Their resident agent was Mr. Kirkwood.

2. Messrs. Hatton and Cookson, general merchants, Liverpool. Their chief agent, Mr. R. B. N. Walker, who had known the river for eleven years (1865), had left a few days before my arrival; his successor, Mr. R. B. Knight, had also sailed for Cape Palmas, to engage Kru-men, and Mr. Hogg had been left in charge.

3. Messrs. Wookey and Dyer, general merchants, Liverpool. Agents, Messrs. Gordon and Bryant.

4. Messrs. Bruford and Townsend, of Bristol. Agent, Captain Townsend.

The resident agents for the Hamburg houses were Messrs. Henert and Bremer.

The English traders in the Gaboon are nominally protected by the Consulate of São Paulo de Loanda, but the distance appears too great for consul or cruizer. They are naturally anxious for some support, and they agitate for an unpaid Consular Agent: at present they have, in African parlance, no "back." A Kruman, offended by a ration of plantains, when he prefers rice, runs to the Plateau, and lays some fictitious complaint before the Commandant. Monsieur summons the merchant, condemns him to pay a fine, and dismisses the affair without even permitting a protest. Hence, impudent robbery occurs every day. The discontent of the white reacts upon his clients the black men; of late, *les Gabons*, as the French call the natives, have gone so far as to declare that foreigners have no right to the upper river, which is all private property. The line drawn by them is at Fetish Rock, off Pointe Française, near the native village of Mpíra, about half a mile above the Plateau; and they would hail with pleasure a transfer to masters who are not so uncommonly ready with their *gros canons*.

The Gaboon trade is chronicled by John Barbot, Agent-General of the French West African Company, "Description of the Coast of South Guinea," Churchill, vol. v. book iv. chap. 9; and the chief items were, and still are, ivory and bees'-wax. Of the former, 90,000 lbs. may be exported when the home prices are good, and sometimes the total has reached 100 tons. Hippopotamus tusks are dying out, being now worth only 2*s*. per lb. Other exports are caoutchouc, ebony (of which the best comes from the Congo), and camwood or barwood (a Tephrosia). M. du Chaillu calls it the "Ego-tree;" the natives (Mpongwe) name the tree Igo, and the billet Ezígo.

CHAPTER II.

THE DEPARTURE.—THE TORNADO.—ARRIVAL AT "THE BUSH."

I SET out early on March 19th, a day, at that time, to me the most melancholy in the year, but now regarded with philosophic indifference. A parting visit to the gallant "Griffons," who threw the slipper, in the shape of three hearty cheers and a "tiger," wasted a whole morning. It was 12.30 P.M. before the mission boat turned her head towards the southern bank, and her crew began to pull in the desultory manner of the undisciplined negro.

The morning had been clear but close, till a fine sea breeze set in unusually early. "The doctor" seldom rises in the Gaboon before noon at this season; often he delays his visit till 2 P.M., and sometimes he does not appear at all. On the other hand, he is fond of late hours. Before we had progressed a mile, suspicious gatherings of slaty-blue cloud-heaps advanced from the north-east against the wind, with a steady and pertinacious speed, showing that mischief was meant. The "cruel, crawling sea" began to rough, purr, and tumble; a heavy cross swell from the south-west dandled the up-torn mangrove twigs, as they floated past us down stream, and threatened to swamp the deeply laden and cranky old boat, which was far off letter A 1 of Lloyd's. The oarsmen became sulky because they were not allowed to make sail, which, in case of a sudden squall, could not have been taken in under half an hour. Patience! Little can be done, on the first day, with these demi-semi-Europeanized Africans, except to succeed in the inevitable trial of strength.

The purple sky-ground backing the Gaboon's upper course admirably set off all its features. Upon the sea horizon, where the river measures some thirty miles across, I could distinctly see the junction of the two main branches, the true Olo' Mpongwe, the main stream flowing from the Eastern Ghats, and the Rembwe (Ramboue) or south-eastern influent. At the confluence, tree-dots, tipping the watery marge, denoted what Barbot calls the "Pongo Islands." These are the quoin-shaped mass "Dámbe" (Orleans Island) *alias* "Coniquet" (the Conelet), often corrupted to Konikey; the Konig Island of the old Hollander,[1]

---

[1] Barbot, book iv. chap. 9.

and the Prince's Island of the ancient Briton. It was so called because held by the Mwáni-pongo, who was to this region what the Mwáni-congo was farther south. The palace was large but very mean, a shell of woven reeds roofed with banana leaves: the people, then mere savages, called their St. James' "Goli-patta," or "Royal House," in imitation of a more civilized race near Cape Lopez. The imperial islet is some six miles in circumference; it was once very well peopled, and here ships used to be careened. The northern point which starts out to meet it is Ovindo (Owëendo of old), *alias* Red Point, *alias* "Rodney's," remarkable for its fair savannah, of which feature more presently. In mid-stream lies Mbini (Embenee), successively Papegay, Parrot—there is one in every Europeo-African river—and Adelaide Island.

Between Ovindo Point, at the northern bend of the stream, stand the so-called "English villages," divided from the French by marshy ground submerged during heavy rains. The highest upstream is Olomi, Otonda-naga, or town of "Cabinda," a son of the late king. Next comes Glass Town, belonging to a dynasty which has lasted a century—longer than many of its European brethren. In 1787 a large ship-bell was sent as a token of regard by a Bristol house, Sydenham and Co., to an old, old "King Glass," whose descendants still reign. Olomi and Glass Town are preferred by the English, as their factories catch the sea-breeze better than can Le Plateau: the nearer swamps are now almost drained off, and the distance from the "authorities" is enough for comfort. Follow Comba (Komba) and Tom Case, the latter called after Case Glass, a scion of the Glasses, who was preferred as captain's "tradesman" by Captain Vidal, R.N., in 1827, because he had "two virtues which rarely fall to the lot of savages, namely, a mild, quiet manner, and a low tone of voice when speaking." Tom Qua Ben, justly proud of the "laced coat of a mail coach guard," was chosen by Captain Boteler, R.N. The list concludes with Butabeya, James Town, and Mpíra.

These villages are not built street-wise after Mpongwe fashion. They are scatters of shabby mat-huts, abandoned after every freeman's death; and they hardly emerge from the luxuriant undergrowth of manioc and banana, sensitive plant and physic nut (Jatropha Curcas), clustering round a palm here and there. Often they are made to look extra mean by a noble "cottonwood," or Bombax (Pentandrium), standing on its stalwart braces like an old sea-dog with parted legs; extending its roots over a square acre of soil, shedding filmy shade upon the surrounding underwood, and at all times ready, like a certain chestnut, to shelter a hundred horses.

Between the Plateau and Santa Clara, beginning

some two miles below the former, are those hated and hating rivals, Louis Town, Qua Ben, and Prince Krinje, the French settlements. The latter is named after a venerable villain who took in every white man with whom he had dealings, till the new colony abolished that exclusive agency, that monopoly so sacred in negro eyes, which here corresponded with the Abbánat of the Somal. Mr. Wilson (p. 252) recounts with zest a notable trick played by this "little, old, grey-headed, humpback man" upon Captain Bouët-Willaumez, and Mr. W. Winwood Reade (chap. xi.) has ably dramatized "Krinji, King George and the Commandant." On another occasion, the whole population of the Gaboon was compelled by a French man-o'-war to pay "Prince Cringy's" debts, and he fell into disfavour only when he attempted to wreck a frigate by way of turning an honest penny.

But soon we had something to think of besides the view. The tumultuous assemblage of dark, dense clouds, resting upon the river-surface in our rear, formed line or rather lines, step upon step, and tier on tier. While the sun shone treacherously gay, a dismal livid gloom palled the eastern sky, descending to the watery horizon; and the estuary, beneath the sable hangings which began to depend from the cloud canopy, gleamed with a ghastly whitish green. Distant thunders rumbled and muttered, and flashes of the broadest sheets inclosed fork and chain lightning; the lift-fire zigzagged in tangled skeins here of chalk-white threads, there of violet wires, to the surface of earth and sea. Presently nimbus-step, tier and canopy, gradually breaking up, formed a low arch regular as the Bifröst bridge which Odin treads, spanning a space between the horizon, ninety degrees broad and more. The sharply cut soffit, which was thrown out in darkest relief by the dim and sallow light of the underlying sky, waxed pendent and ragged, as though broken by a torrent of storm. What is technically called the "ox-eye," the "egg of the tornado," appeared in a fragment of space, glistening below the gloomy rain-arch. The wind ceased to blow; every sound was hushed as though Nature were nerving herself, silent for the throe, and our looks said, "In five minutes it will be down upon us." And now it comes. A cold blast smelling of rain, and a few drops or rather splashes, big as gooseberries and striking with a blow, are followed by a howling squall, sharp and sudden puffs, pulsations and gusts; at length a steady gush like a rush of steam issues from that awful arch, which, after darkening the heavens like an eclipse, collapses in fragmentary torrents of blinding rain. In the midst of the spoon-drift we see, or we think we see, "La Junon" gliding like a phantom-ship towards the river mouth. The lightning seems to work its way into our eyes, the air-shaking thunder rolls and roars around our very ears; the oars are taken in utterly useless, the storm-wind sweeps the boat before it at full speed as though it had been a bit of straw. Selim and I sat with a large mackintosh sheet over our hunched backs, thus offering a breakwater to the waves; happily for us, the billow-heads were partly cut off and carried away bodily by the raging wind, and the opened fountains of the firmament beat down the breakers before they could grow to their full growth. Otherwise we were lost men; the southern shore was still two miles distant, and, as it was, the danger was not despicable. These tornadoes are harmless enough to a cruiser, and under a good roof men bless them. But H.M.S. "Heron" was sunk by one, and the venture of a cranky gig laden *à fleur d'eau* is what some call "tempting Providence."

Stunned with thunder, dazzled by the vivid flashes of white lightning, dizzy with the drive of the boat, and drenched by the torrents and washings from above and below, we were not a little pleased to feel the storm-wind slowly lulling, as it had cooled the heated regions ahead, and to see the sky steadily clearing up behind, as the blackness of the cloud, rushing with racer speed, passed over and beyond us.

The increasing stillness of the sea raised our spirits;

> "For nature, only loud when she destroys,
> Is silent when she fashions."

But the storm-demon's name is "Tornado" (Cyclone): it will probably veer round to the south, where, meeting the dry clouds that are gathering and massing there, it will involve us in another fray. Meanwhile we are safe, and as the mist clears off we sight the southern shore. The humbler elevation, notably different from the northern bank, is dotted with villages and clearings. The Péninsule de Marie-Amélie, *alias* "Round Corner," the innermost southern point visible from the mouth, projects to the north-north-east in a line of scattered islets at high tides, ending in *Le bois Fétiche*, a clump of tall trees somewhat extensively used for picnics. It has served for worse purposes, as the name shows.

A total of two hours landed me from the Comte de Paris Roads upon the open sandy strip that supports Denistown; the single broad street runs at right angles from the river, the better to catch the sea-breeze, and most of the huts have open gables, a practice strongly to be recommended. *Le Roi* would not expose himself to the damp air; the consul was not so particular. His majesty's levée took place in the verandah of a poor bamboo hut, one of the dozen which compose his capital. Seated in a chair and ready for business, he was surrounded by a crowd of courtiers, who listened attentively to every word, especially when he affected to whisper; and some pretty women collected to peep round the corners at the *Utangáni* (white man).[1]

Mr. Wilson described Roi Denis in 1856 as a man of middle stature, with compact frame and well-made, of great muscular power, about sixty years old, very black by contrast with the snow-white beard veiling his brown face. "He has a mild and expressive eye, a gentle and persuasive voice, equally affable and dignified; and, taken altogether, he is one of the most king-like looking men I have ever met in Africa," says the reverend gentleman. The account reminded me of Kimwere the Lion of Usumbara, drawn by Dr. Krapf. Perhaps six years had exercised a degeneratory effect upon Roi Denis, or perchance I have more realism than sentiment; my eyes could see nothing but a *petit vieux vieux*, nearer sixty than seventy, with a dark, wrinkled face, and an uncommonly crafty eye, one of those African organs

---

[1] This word is the Muzungu of the Zanzibar coast, and contracted to Utángá and even Tángá it is found useful in expressing foreign wares; Utangáni's devil-fire, for instance, is a lucifer match.

which is always occupied in "taking your measure" not for your good.

I read out the introductory letter from Baron Didelot—the king speaks a little French and English, but of course his education ends there.

THE AFRICAN KING.

After listening to my projects and to my offers of dollars, liquor, and cloth, Roi Denis replied, with due gravity, that his chasseurs were all in the plantations, but that for a somewhat increased consideration he would attach to my service his own son Ogodembe, *alias* Paul. It was some time before I found out the real meaning of this crafty move; the sharp prince, sent to do me honour, intended me to recommend him to Mr. Hogg as an especially worthy recipient of "trust." Roi Denis added an abundance of "sweet mouf," and, the compact ended, he condescendingly walked down with me to the beach, shook hands and exchanged a civilized "Au revoir." I re-entered the boat, and we pushed off once more.

Prince Paul, a youth of the Picaresque school, a hungry as well as a thirsty soul and vain with knowledge, which we know "puffeth up," having the true African eye on present gain as well as to future "trust," proceeded: "Papa has at least a hundred sons," enough to make Dan Dinmont blush, "and say" (he was not sure), "a hundred and fifty daughters. Father rules all the southern shore; the French have no power beyond the brack and there are no African rivals,"—the prince evidently thought that the new-comer had never heard of King George. Like most juniors here, the youth knew French, or rather Gaboon-French; it was somewhat startling to hear clearly and tolerably pronounced, "M'sieur, veux-tu des macacques?" But the jargon is not our S'a Leone and West-coast "English;" the superior facility of pronouncing the neo-Latin tongues became at once apparent. It is evident that European languages have been a mistake in

Africa: the natives learn a smattering sufficient for business purposes and foreigners remain without the key to knowledge; hence our small progress in understanding negro human nature. Had we so acted in British India, we should probably have held the proud position which now contents us in China as in Western Africa, with factories and hulks at Bombay, Calcutta, Karachí, and Madras.

From Comte de Paris Roads the southern Gaboon shore is called in charts Le Paletuvier, the Mangrove Bank; the rhizophora is the growth of shallow brackish water, and at the projections there are fringings of reefs and "diabolitos," dangerous to boats. After two hours we crossed the Mombe (Mombay) Creek-mouth, with its outlying rocks, and passed the fishing village of Nenga-Oga, whence supplies are sent daily to the Plateau. Then doubling a point of leek-green grass, based upon comparatively poor soil, sand, and clay, and backed by noble trees, we entered the Mbátá River, the Toutiay of the chart and the Batta Creek of M. du Chaillu's map. It comes from the south-west, and it heads much nearer the coast than is shown on paper.

Presently the blood-red sun sank like a fire-balloon into the west, flushing with its last fierce beams the higher clouds of the eastern sky, and lighting the white and black plume of the soaring fish-eagle. This Gypohierax (Angolensis) is a very wild bird, flushed at 200 yards: I heard of, but I never saw, the Gwanyoni, which M. du Chaillu, (chapter xvi.) calls Guanionian, an eagle or a vulture said to kill deer. Rain fell at times, thunder, anything but "sweet thunder," again rolled in the distance; and lightning flashed and forked before and behind us, becoming painfully vivid in the shades darkening apace. We could see nothing of the channel but a steel-grey streak, like a Damascus blade, in a sable sheathing of tall mangrove avenue; in places, however, tree-clumps suggested delusive hopes that we were approaching a region where man can live. On our return we found many signs of population which had escaped our sight during the fast-growing obscurity. The first two reaches were long and bulging; the next became shorter, and Prince Paul assured us that, after one to the right, and another to the left, we should fall into the direct channel. Roi Denis had promised us arrival at sunset; his son gradually protracted sunset till midnight. Still the distance grew and grew. I now learned for the first time that the boat was too large for the channel, and that oars were perfectly useless ahead.

At 8 P.M. we entered what seemed a *cul de sac;* it looked like charging a black wall, except where a gleam of grey light suggested the further end of the Box Tunnel, and cheered our poor hearts for a short minute, whilst in the distance we heard the tantalizing song of the wild waves. The boughs on both sides brushed the boat; we held our hands before our faces to avoid the sharp stubs threatening ugly stabs, and to fend off the low branches, ready to sweep us and our belongings into the deep swirling water. The shades closed in like the walls of the Italian's dungeon; until our eyes grew to it, the blackness of Erebus weighed upon our spirits; perspiration poured from our brows, and in this watery mangrove-lane the *pabulum vitæ* seemed to be wanting. After forcing a passage through three vile "gates," the sheet-lightning announced a second tornado. We sighed for more vivid flashes, but after twenty minutes they dimmed and died away, still showing the "bush"-silhouette on either side. The tide rushed out in strength under the amphibious forest—all who know the West Coast will appreciate the position. It was impossible to advance or to remain in this devil's den, the gig bumped at every minute, and the early flood would probably crush her against the trees. So we dropped down to the nearest "open," which we reached at 9.30 P.M.

After enduring a third tornado we grounded, and the crew sprang ashore, saying that they were going to boil plantains on the bank. I made snug for the night with a wet waterproof and a strip of muslin, to be fastened round the mouth after the fashion of Outram's "fever guard," and shut my lips to save my life, by the particular advice of Dr. Catlin. The first mosquito piped his "Io Pæan" at 8 P.M.; another hour brought legions, and then began the battle for our blood. I had resolved not to sleep in the fetid air of the jungle; time, however, moved on wings of lead; a dull remembrance of a watery moon, stars dimly visible, a southerly breeze, and heavy drops falling from the trees long haunted me. About midnight, Prince Paul, who had bewailed the hardship of passing a night *sans mostiquaire* in the bush, and whose violent plungings showed that he failed to manage *un somme*, proposed to land and to fetch fire from *l'habitation.*

"What habitation?"

"Oh! a little village belonging to papa."

"And why the —— didn't you mention it?"

"Ah! this is Mponbinda, and you know we're bound for Mbátá!"

Nothing negrotic now astonishes us, there is nought new to me in Africa. We landed upon a natural pier of rock ledge, and, after some 400 yards of good path, we entered a neat little village, and found our crew snoring snugly asleep. We "exhorted them," refreshed the fire, and generously recruited exhausted nature with quinine, julienne and tea, potatoes and potted meats, pipes and cigars. So sped my annual unlucky day, and thus was spent my first jungle-night almost exactly under the African line.

At 5 A.M. the new morning dawned, the young tide flowed, the crabs disappeared, and the gig, before high and dry on the hard mud, once more became buoyant. Forward again! The channel was a labyrinthine ditch, an interminable complication of over-arching roots, and of fallen trees forming gateways; the threshold was a maze of slimy stumps, stems, and forks in every stage of growth and decay, dense enough to exclude the air of heaven. In parts there were ugly snags, and everywhere the turns were so puzzling, that I marvelled how a human being could attempt the passage by night. The best time for ascending is half-flood, for descending half-ebb; if the water be too high, the bush chokes the way; if too low, the craft grounds. At the Gaboon mouth the tide rises three feet; at the head of the Mbátá Creek, where it arrests the sweet water rivulet, it is, of course, higher.

And now the scene improved. The hat-palm, a brab or wild date, the spine-palm (*Phœnix spinosa*), and the Okumeh or cotton-tree disputed the ground with the foul Rhizophora. Then clearings appeared. At Ejéné, the second of two landing-places evidently leading to farms, we transferred ourselves to canoes, our boat being arrested by a fallen tree. Advancing a few yards, all disembarked upon trampled mud, and, ascending the bank, left the creek which supplies baths and drinking water to our destination. Striking a fair pathway, we passed westward over a low wave of ground, sandy and mouldy, and traversed a fern field surrounded by a forest of secular trees; some parasite-grown from twig to root, others blanched and scathed by the fires of heaven; these roped and corded with runners and llianas, those naked and clothed in motley patches. At 6.30 A.M., after an hour's work, probably representing a mile, and a total of 7 h. 30 m., or six miles in a south-south-west direction from Le Plateau, we left the ugly *cul de sac* of a creek, and entered Mbátá, which the French call "La Plantation."

Women and children fled in terror at our approach—and no wonder: eyes like hunted boars, haggard faces, yellow as the sails at the Cape Verdes, and beards two days long, act very unlike cosmetics. Ahouse was cleared for us by Hotaloya, *alias* "Andrew," of the Baráka Mission, the lord of the village, who, poor fellow! has only two wives; he is much ashamed of himself, but his excuse is, "I be boy now," meaning about twenty-two. After breakfast we prepared for a sleep, but the popular excitement forbade it; the villagers had heard that a white greenhorn was coming to bag and to buy gorillas, and they resolved to make hay whilst the sun shone.

Prince Paul at once gathered together a goodly crowd of fathers and mothers, uncles and aunts, brothers and sisters, cousins and connections. A large and loud-voiced dame, "Gozeli," swore that she was his "proper Ngwe," being one of his numerous step-mas, and she would not move without a head, or three leaves, of tobacco. Hotaloya was his brother; Mesdames Azízeh and Asúnye

THE HUNTER AND HIS TWO WIVES.

declared themselves his sisters, and so all. My little stock of goods began visibly to shrink, when I informed the greedy applicants that nothing beyond a leaf of tobacco and a demi-verre of *tafia* would be given until I had seen my way to work. Presently appeared the chief huntsman appointed by Roi Denis to take charge of me; he was named Fortuna, a Spanish name corrupted to Forteune. A dash was then prepared for his majesty and for Prince Paul: I regret to say that this young nobleman ended his leave-taking by introducing a pretty woman, with very neat hands and ankles and a most *mutine* physiognomy, as his sister, informing me that she was also my wife *pro temp.* She did not seem likely to *coiffer Sainte Cathérine*, and here she is.

PRINCE PAUL'S SISTER.

The last thing the prince did was to carry off, without a word of leave, the mission boat and the three Kru-boys, whom he kept two days. I was uneasy about these fellows, who, hating and fearing the Gaboon "bush," are ever ready to bolt.

Forteune and Hotaloya personally knew Mpolo (Paul du Chaillu), and often spoke to me of his prowess as a chasseur and his knowledge of their tongue. But reputation as a linguist is easily made in these regions by speaking a few common sentences. The gorilla-hunter evidently had only a colloquial acquaintance with the half-dozen various idioms of the Mpongwe and Mpáńgwe (Fá*n*) Bakĕle, Shekyani, and Cape Lopez people. Yet, despite verbal inaccuracies, his facility of talking gave him immense advantages over other whites, chiefly in this, that the natives would deem it useless to try the usual tricks upon travellers.

Forteune is black, short, and "trapu;" curls of the jettiest lanugo invest all his outward man; bunches of muscle stand out from his frame like the statues of Crotonian Milo; his legs are bandy; his hands and feet are large and patulous, and he wants only a hunch to make an admirable Quasimodo. He has the frank and open countenance of a sportsman—I had been particularly warned by the Plateau folk about his skill in cheating and lying. Formerly a cook at the Gaboon, he is a man of note in his tribe, as the hunter always is; he holds the position of a country gentleman, who can afford to write himself M. F. H.; he is looked upon as a man of valour; he is admired by the people, and he is adored by his wives—one of them at once took up her station upon the marital knee. Perhaps the Nimrod of Mbátá is just a little henpecked—the Mpongwe mostly are—and I soon found out that *soigner les femmes* is the royal road to getting on with the men. He supplies the village with "beef," here meaning not the roast of Old England, but any meat, from a field-rat to a hippopotamus. He boasts that he has slain with his own hand upwards of a hundred gorillas and anthropoid apes, and, since the demand arose in Europe, he has supplied Mr. R. B. N. Walker and others with an average of one per month, including a live youngster; probably most, if not all, of them were killed by his "bushmen," of whom he can command about a dozen.

Forteune began by receiving his "dash," six fathoms of "satin cloth," tobacco, and pipes. After inspecting my battery, he particularly approved of a smooth-bored double-barrel (Beattie of Regent Street) carrying six to the pound. Like all these people, he uses an old and rickety trade-musket, and, when lead is wanting, he loads it with a bit of tile: as many gorillas are killed with tools which would hardly bring down a wild cat, it is evident that their vital power cannot be great. He owned to preferring a charge of twenty buck-shot to a single ball, and he received with joy a little fine gunpowder, which he compared complimentarily with the blasting article, half charcoal withal, to which he was accustomed.

Presently a decently dressed, white-bearded man of light complexion announced himself, with a flourish and a loud call for a chair, as Prince

Koyálá, *alias* "Young Prince," father to Forteune and Hotaloya and brother to Roi Denis,—here all tribesmen are of course brethren. This being equivalent to "asking for more," it drove me to the limits of my patience. It was evidently now necessary to assume wrath, and to raise my voice to a roar.

"My hands dey be empty! I see nuffin, I hear nuffin! What for I make more dash?"

Allow me, parenthetically, to observe that the African, like the Scotch Highlander, will interpose the personal or demonstrative pronoun between noun and verb: "sun he go down," means "the sun sets" and, as genders do not exist, you must be careful to say, "This woman he cry too much."

The justice of my remark was owned by all; had it been the height of tyranny, the supple knaves would have agreed with me quite as politely. They only replied that "Young Prince," being a man of years and dignity, would be dishonoured by dismissal empty-handed, and they represented him as my future host when we moved nearer the bush.

"Now lookee here. This he be bad plábbá (palaver). This he be bob! I come up for white man, you come up for black man. All white man he no be fool, 'cos he no got black face!"

Ensued a chorus of complimentary palaver

touching the infinite superiority of the Aryan over the Semite, but the point was in no wise yielded. At last Young Prince subsided into a request for a glass of rum, which being given "cut the palaver" (*i.e.* ended the business). I soon resolved to show my hosts, by threatening to leave them, the difference between traders and travellers. Barbot relates that the Mpongwe of olden time demanded his "dassy" before he consented to "liquor up," and boldly asked, "If he was expected to drink gratis?" The impertinence was humoured, otherwise not an ivory would have found its way to the factory. But the traveller is not bound to endure these whimsy-whamsies; and the sooner he declares his independence the better. Many monkeys' skins were brought to me for sale, but I refused to buy, lest the people might think it my object to make money; moreover, all were spoilt for specimens by the "points" being snipped off.

I happened during the first afternoon to show my hosts a picture of the bald-headed chimpanzee, Nchígo Mbúwwe (*Troglodytes calvus*), here more generally called Nchígo Mpolo, "large chimpanzee," or Nchígo Njúe, "white-haired chimpanzee." They recognized it at once; but when I turned over to the cottage ("Adventures," &c., p. 423), with its neat parachute-like roof, all burst out laughing.

"You want to look him Nágo (house)?" asked Hotaloya.

"Yes, for sure," I replied.

Forteune set out at once, carrying my gun, Selim followed me, and the rear was brought up by a couple of little prick-eared curs with a dash of the pointer, probably from St. Helena: the people will pay as much as ten dollars for a good dog. They are never used in hunting apes, as they start the game; on this occasion they nearly ran down a small antelope.

The path led through a new clearing; a field of fern and some patches of grass breaking the forest, which, almost clear of thicket and undergrowth, was a charming place for deer. The soil, thin sand overlying humus, suggested rich crops of ground-nuts; its surface was everywhere cut by nullahs, now dry, and by brooks, running crystal streams; these, when deep, are crossed by tree-trunks, the Brazilian "pingela." After twenty minutes or so we left the "picada" (foot-path) and struck into a thin bush, till we had walked about a mile.

"Look him house, Nchígo house!" said Hotaloya, standing under a tall tree.

I saw to my surprise two heaps of dry sticks, which a schoolboy might have taken for birds' nests; the rude beds, boughs, torn off from the tree, not gathered, were built in forks, one ten and the other twenty feet above ground, and both were canopied by the tufted tops. Every hunter consulted upon the subject ridiculed the branchy roof tied with vines, and declared that the Nchígo's industry is confined to a place for sitting, not for shelter; that he fashions no other dwelling; that a couple generally occupies the same or some neighbouring tree, each sitting upon its own nest; that the Nchígo is not a "hermit" nor a rare, nor even a very timid animal; that it dwells, as I saw, near villages, and that its cry, "Aoo! Aoo! Aoo!" is often heard by them in the mornings and evenings. During my subsequent wanderings in Gorilla land, I often observed tall and mushroom-shaped trees standing singly, and wearing the semblance of the umbrella roof. What most puzzles me is, that M. du Chaillu ("Second Expedition," chap. iii.) "had two of the bowers cut down and sent to the British Museum." He adds, "They are formed at a height of twenty to thirty feet in the trees, by the animals bending over and intertwining a number of the weaker boughs, so as to form bowers, under which they can sit, protected from the rains by the masses of foliage thus entangled together, some of the boughs being so bent that they form convenient seats." Surely M. du Chaillu must have been deceived by some vagary of nature.

The gorilla-hunter's sketch had always reminded me of the Rev. Mr. Moffat's account of the Hylobian Bakones, the aborigines of the Matabele country. Mr. Thompson, a missionary to Sherbro ("The Palm Land," chap. xiii), has, however, these words:—"It is said of the chimpanzees, that they build a kind of rude house of sticks in their wild state, and fill it with leaves; and I doubt it not, for when domesticated they always want some good bed, and make it up regularly."

Thus I come to the conclusion that the Nchígo Mpolo is a vulgar nest-building ape. The bushmen and the villagers all assured me that neither the common chimpanzee, nor the gorilla proper (*Troglodytes gorilla*), "make 'im house." On the other hand, Mr. W. Winwood Reade, writing to "The Athenæum" from Loanda (Sept. 7, 1862), asserts,—"When the female is pregnant he (the gorilla) builds a nest (as do also the Kulu-Kamba and the chimpanzee), where she is delivered, and which is then abandoned." And he thus confirms what was told to Dr. Thomas Savage (1847): "In the wild state their (*i.e.* the gorillas') habits are in general like those of the *Troglodytes niger*, building their nests loosely in trees."

CHAPTER III.

GEOGRAPHY OF THE GABOON.

EFORE going further afield I may be allowed a few observations, topographical and ethnological, about this highly interesting section of the West African coast.

The Gaboon country, to retain the now familiar term, although no one knows much about its derivation, is placed by old travellers in "South Guinea," the tract lying along the Ethiopic, or South Atlantic Ocean, limited by the Camarones Mountain-block in north latitude 4°, and by Cabo Negro in south latitude 15° 40′ 7″, a sea-line of nearly 1,200 miles. The Gaboon proper is included between the Camarones Mountains to the north, and the "Mayumba," properly the "Yumba" country southwards, in south latitude 3° 22′,—a shore upwards of 400 miles long. The inland depth is undetermined; geographically we should limit it to the Western Ghats, which rarely recede more than 60 miles from the sea, and ethnologically no line can yet be drawn. The country is almost bisected by the equator, and by the Rio de Gabão, which discharges in north latitude 0° 21′ 25″ and east longitude 9° 21′ 23″; and it corresponds in parallel with the Somali-Galla country and the Juba River on the east coast.

The general aspect of the region is prepossessing. It is a rolling surface sinking towards the Atlantic, in parts broken by hills and dwarf chains, either detached or pushed out by the Ghats; a land of short and abnormally broad rivers, which cannot, like the Congo, break through the ridges flanking the Central African basin, and which therefore are mere surface drains of the main ranges. The soil is mostly sandy, but a thin coat of rich vegetable humus, quickened by heavy rains and fiery suns, produces a luxuriant vegetation; whilst the proportion of area actually cultivated is nothing compared with the expanse of bush. In the tall forests, which abound in wild fruits, there are beautiful tracts of clear grassy land, and the woods, clear of undergrowth, resemble an English grove more than a tropical jungle. Horses, which die of the tsetse (*Glossina morsitans*) in the interior of North Guinea, and of damp heat at Fernando Po, thrive on its downs and savannahs. The Elaïs palm is rare, sufficing only for home use. The southern parts, about Cape Lopez and beyond it, resemble the Oil River country in the Biafran Bight: the land is a mass of mangrove swamps, and the climate is unfit for white men.

The Eastern Ghats were early known to the "Iberians," as shown by the Sierra del Crystal, del Sal, del Sal Nitro and other names, probably so called from the abundance of quartz in blocks and veins that seam the granite, as we shall see in the Congo country, and possibly because they contain rock crystal. Although in many places they may be descried subtending the shore in lumpy lines like detached vertebræ, and are supposed to represent the Aranga Mons of Ptolemy, they are not noticed by Barbot. Between the Camarones River and Cape St. John (Corisco Bay), blue, rounded, and discontinuous masses, apparently wooded, rise before the mariner, and form, as will be seen, the western sub-ranges of the great basin-rim. To the north they probably anastomose with the Camarones, the Rumbi, the Kwa, the Fumbina north-east, and the Niger-Kong mountains.[1]

They are not wanting who declare them to be rich in precious metals. Some thirty years ago an American super-cargo ascended the Rembwe River, the south-eastern line of the Gaboon fork, and is said to have collected "dirt" which, tested

---

"Abeokuta and the Camaroons Mountains," vol. ii. chap. i. London: Tinsleys, 1863.

at New York, produced 16 dollars per bushel. All the old residents in the Gaboon know the story of the gold dust. The prospector was the late Captain Richard E. Lawlin, of New York, who was employed by Messrs. Bishop of Philadelphia, the same house that commissioned the *chasseur de gorilles* to collect "rubber" for them, and who was so eminently useful to the young French traveller

SIERRA DEL CRYSTAL, FROM THE SEA.

that the scant notice of his name is considered curious.

Great would be my wonder if the West African as well as the East African Ghats did not prove auriferous; both fulfil all the required conditions, and both await actual discovery. The Mountains of the Moon, so frequently mentioned by M. du Chaillu and the Gaboon Mission, are doubtless the versants between the valleys of the Niger and the Congo. Lately Dr. Schweinfurth found an equatorial range which, stretching northwards towards the Bahr el

Ghazal, was seen to trend westward. According to Mr. Consul Hutchinson ("Ten Years' Wanderings among the Ethiopians," p. 250), the Rev. Messrs. Mackey and Clemens, of the Corisco Mission "explored more than a hundred miles of country across the Sierra del Crystal Range of Mountains"—I am inclined to believe that a hundred miles from the coast was their furthest point. We shall presently travel towards this mysterious range, and there is no difficulty in passing it, except the utter want of a commercial road, and the wildness of tribes that have never sighted a traveller nor a civilized man.

The rivers of our region are of three kinds; little surface drains principally in the north; broad estuaries like the Mersey and many streams of Eastern Scotland in the central parts, and a single bed, the Ogobe, breaking through the subtending Ghats, and forming a huge lagoon-delta. Beginning at Camarones are the Boroa and Borba Waters, with the Rio de Campo, fifteen leagues further south; of these little is known, except that they fall into the Bight of Panari or Pannaria.

According to Barbot (iv. 9), the English charts give the name of Point Pan to a large deep bight in which lies the harbour-bay "Porto de Garapo" (Garápa, sugar-cane juice?); and he calls the two rounded hillocks, extending inland from Point Pan to the northern banks of the Rio de Campo,

"Navia." The un-African word Panari or Pannaria is probably a corruption of Páo de Nao, the bay north of Garapo, and "Navia."

These small features are followed by the Rio de São Bento, improperly called in our charts the St. Benito, Bonito, Bonita, and Boneto; the native name is Lobei, and it traverses the Kombi country, —such is the extent of our information. The next is the well-known Muni, the Ntambounay of M. du Chaillu, generally called the Danger River, in old charts "Rio de São João," and "Rio da Angra" (of the bight); an estuary which, like most of its kind, bifurcates above, and, receiving a number of little tributaries from the Sierra, forms a broad bed and empties itself through a mass of mangroves into the innermost north-eastern corner of Corisco Bay. This sag in the coast is formed by Ninje (Nenge the island?), or the Cabo de São João (Cape St. John) to the north, fronted south by a large square-headed block of land, whose point is called Cabo das Esteiras—of matting (Barbot's Estyras), an article of trade in the olden time. The southern part receives the Munda (Moondah) river, a foul and unimportant stream, which has been occupied by the American missionaries.

We shall ascend the Gaboon estuary to its sources. South of it, a number of sweet little water-courses break the shore-line as far as the Nazareth River, which debouches north of Urungu, or Cape Lopez (Cabo de Lopo Gonsalvez), and which forms by anastomosing with a southern river the Ogobe (Ogowai of M. du Chaillu), a complicated delta whose sea-front extends from north to south, at least eighty miles. Beyond Cape Lopez is an outfall, known to Europeans as the Rio Mexias : it is apparently a mesh in the net-work of the Nazareth-Ogobe. The same may be said of the Rio Fernão Vaz, about 110 miles south of the Gaboon, and of yet another stream which, running lagoon-like some forty miles along the shore, has received in our maps the somewhat vague name of R. Rembo or River River. Orembo (Simpongwe) being the generic term for a stream or river, is applied emphatically to the Nkomo branch of the Gaboon, and to the Fernão Vaz.

The Ogobe is the only river between the Niger and the Congo which escapes, through favouring depressions, from the highlands flanking the great watery plateau of Inner Africa. By its plainly marked double seasons of flood at the equinoxes, and by the time of its low water, we prove that it drains the belt of calms, and the region immediately upon the equator. The explorations of Lieutenant Serval and others, in "Le Pionnier" river-steamer, give it an average breadth of 8,200 feet, though broken by sand-banks and islands; the depth in the main channel, which at times is narrow and difficult to find, averages between sixteen and forty-eight feet; and, in the dry season of 1862, the vessel ran up sixty English miles.

Before M. du Chaillu's expeditions, "the rivers known to Europeans," he tells us in his Preface ("First Journey," p. iv.), "as the Nazareth, Mexias, and Fernam Vaz, were supposed to be three distinct streams." In 1817 Bowdich identified the "Ogoowai" with the Congo, and the Rev. Mr. Wilson (p. 284) shows us the small amount of knowledge that existed even amongst experts, five years before the "Gorilla book" appeared. "From Cape Lopez, where the Nazareth debouches, there is a narrow lagoon running along the sea-coast, and very near to it, all the way to Mayumba. This lagoon is much traversed by boats and canoes, and, when the slave-trade was in vigorous operation, it afforded the Portuguese traders great facilities for eluding the vigilance of British cruizers, by shifting their slaves from point to point, and embarking them, according to a preconcerted plan."

M. du Chaillu first proved that the Ogobe was formed by two forks, the northern, or Rembo Okanda, and the southern, or Rembo Nguye. The former is the more important. Mr. R. S. N. Walker found this stream above the confluence to be from 1,800 to 2,100 feet wide, though half the bed was occupied by bare sand-banks. Higher up, where rocks and rapids interfered with the boat-voyage, the current was considerable, but the breadth diminished to 600 feet. The southern branch (also written Ngunië) was found in Apono Land (S. lat. 2°), about the breadth of the Thames at London Bridge, 700 feet. In June the depth was ten to fifteen feet, to which the rainy season added ten.

M. du Chaillu also established the facts that the Nazareth river was the northern arm of the Delta, and that the Fernão Vaz anastomosed with the Delta's southern arm.

The only pelagic islands off the Gaboon coast are the Brancas, Great and Little; Corisco Island, which we shall presently visit; Great and Little Elobi, called by old travellers Mosquito Islands, probably for "Moucheron," a Dutchman who lost his ship there in 1600. The land about the mouths of the Ogobe is a mass of mangrove swamps, like the Nigerian Delta, which high tides convert into insular ground; these, however, must be considered *terra firma* in its infancy. The riverine islands of the Gaboon proper will be noticed as we ascend the bed.

Pongo-land ignores all such artificial partitions as districts or parishes; the only divisions are the countries occupied by the several tribes.

The Gaboon lies in "Africa-on-the-Line," and a description of the year at Zanzibar Island applies to it in many points.[1] The characteristic of this equatorial belt is uniformity of temperature: whilst the Arabian and the Australian deserts often show a variation of 50° Fahr. in a single day, the yearly range of the mercury at Singapore is about 10°. The four seasons of the temperates are utterly unknown to the heart of the tropics—even in Hindostan the poet who would sing, for instance, the charms of spring must borrow the latter word (Buhar) from the Persian. If the "bull" be allowed, the only rule here appears to be one of exceptions. The traveller is always assured that this time there have been no rains, or no dries, or no tornadoes, or one or all in excess, till at last he comes to the conclusion that the Clerk of the Weather must have mislaid his ledger. Contrary to the popular idea, which has descended to us from the classics, the climate under the Line is not of that torrid heat which a vertical sun suggests; the burning zone of the Old World begins in the northern hemisphere, where the regular rains do not extend, beyond the tenth as far as the twenty-fifth degree. The equatorial climate is essentially temperate: for instance, the heat of Sumatra, lying almost under the Line, rarely exceeds 24° R. = 86° Fahr. In the Gaboon the thermometer ranges from 65° to 90° Fahr., "a degree of heat,"

---

[1] See "Zanzibar City, Island, and Coast," vol. i. chap. v sect. 2.

says Dr. Ford, "less than in many salubrious localities in other parts of the world."

Upon the Gaboon the wet seasons are synchronous with the vertical suns at the vernal and autumnal equinoxes. "The rainy season of a place within the tropics always begins when the sun has reached the zenith of that place. Then the trade-winds, blowing regularly at other seasons, become gradually weaker, and at length cease and give way to variable winds and calms. The trade-wind no longer brings its regular supply of cooler, drier air; the rising heats and calms favour an ascending current" (in the sea-depths, I may add, as well as on land), "which bears the damp air into the upper regions of the atmosphere, there to be cooled, and to occasion the heavy down-pour of each afternoon. The nights and mornings are for the most part bright and clear. When the sun moves away from the zenith, the trade-winds again begin to be felt, and bring with them the dry season of the year, during which hardly ever a cloud disturbs the serenity of the skies.

"Between the tropical limits and the equator, however, the sun comes twice to the zenith of each place. If now, between the going and coming of the sun, from the Line to its furthest range, a sufficient pause intervenes, or if the sun's temporary distance from the zenith is great enough, the rainy season is divided into two portions, separated by a lesser dry season. Closer to the tropical lines, where the sun remains but once in the zenith, the rainy season is a continuous one."

Such is the theory of the "Allgemeine Erdkunde" (Hahn, Hochstetter and Pokorny, Prague, 1872). An explanation should be added of the reason why the cool wind ceases to blow, at the time when the air, heated and raised by a perpendicular sun, might be expected to cause a greater indraught. We at once, I have said, recognize its correctness at sea. The Gaboon, "in the belt of calms, with rain during the whole year," has two distinctly marked dry seasons, at the vernal and the autumnal equinoxes. The former or early rains (Nchangyá?) are expected to begin in February, with violent tornadoes and storms, especially at the full and change, and to end in April. The heavy downfalls are mostly at night, possibly an effect of the Sierra del Crystal. I found March 28th (1862) very like damp weather at the end of an English May; April 6th was equally exceptional, raining from dawn to evening. During my trip to Sánga-Tánga and back (March 25th to 29th) we had frequent fogs, locally called "smokes," and almost daily tornadoes, sometimes from the south-east, whilst the lightning was dangerous as upon the Western prairies. After an interval of fiery sun, with occasional rain torrents and discharges of electricity, begin the Enomo (Enun?), the "middle" or long dries, which last four months to September. The "Enomo" is the Angolan Cacimbo, meaning cool and cloudy weather, when no umbrella is required, and when the invariably grey sky rarely rains. Travellers are told that June and July are the cream of the year, the healthiest time for seasoned Europeans, and this phantom of a winter renders the climate more supportable to the northern constitution.

During the "middle dries," when the sun, retiring to the summer solstice, is most distant, land winds and sea breezes are strong and regular, and the people suffer severely from cold. In the Gaboon heavy showers sometimes fall, July being the least subject to them, and the fiery sun, when it can disperse the clouds, turns the soil to dust. At the end of September appear the "latter rains," which are the more copious, as they seldom last more than six hours at a time. It is erroneous to assert that "the tract nearest the equator on both sides has the longest rainy season;" the measure chiefly depends upon altitude and other local conditions.

The rainy seasons are healthier for the natives than the cold seasons; and the explorer is often urged to take advantage of them. He must, however, consult local experience. Whilst ascending rivers in November, for instance, he may find the many feet of flood a boon or a bane, and his marching journeys are nearly sure to end in ulcerated feet, as was the case with poor Dr. Livingstone. The rains drench the country till the latter end of December, when the Nángá or "little dries" set in for two months. The latter also are not unbroken by storms and showers, and they end with tornadoes, which this year (1862) have been unusually frequent and violent. Thus we may distribute the twelve months into six of rains, vernal and autumnal, and six of dry weather, æstival and hibernal: the following table will show the sub-sections:—

Early December to early February, the "little dries;" February to early April, the "former," early or spring rains; May to early June, the variable weather; June to early September, the Cacimbo, Enomo, long or middle dries; September to early December, the "latter rains."

Under such media the disease, *par excellence*, of the Gaboon is the paroxysm which is variously called Coast, African, Guinea, and Bullom fever. Dr. Ford, who has written a useful treatise upon the subject,[1] finds hebdomadal peri-

---

[1] "Observations on the Fevers of the West African Coast." New York: Jenkins, 1856. A more valuable work is the "Medical Topography, &c. of West Africa," by the late W. F. Daniell, M.D., 1849. Finally, Mr. Consul Hutchinson offered valuable suggestions in his work on the Niger Expedition of 1854-5 (Longmans, 1855, and republished in the "Traveller's Library").

odicity in the attacks, and lays great stress upon this point of chronothermalism. He recognizes the normal stages, preparatory, invasional, reactionary, and resolutionary. Like Drs. Livingstone and Hutchinson, he holds fever and quinine "incompatibles," and he highly approves of the prophylactic adhibition of chinchona used by the unfortunate Douville in 1828. Experience in his own person and in numerous patients "proves all theoretical objections to the use of six grains an hour, or fifty and sixty grains of quinine in one day or remission to be absolutely imaginary." He is "convinced that it is not a stimulant," and with many apologies he cautiously sanctions alcohol, which should often be the physician's mainstay. As he advocated ten-grain doses of calomel by way of preliminary cathartic, the American missionaries stationed on the River have adopted a treatment still more "severe"—quinine till deafness ensues, and half a handful of mercury, often continued till a passage opens through the palate, placing mouth and nose in directer communication. Dr. Ford also recommends during the invasion or period of chills external friction of mustard or of fresh red pepper either in tincture or in powder, a good alleviator always procurable; and the internal use of pepper-tea, to bring on the stages of reaction and resolution. Few will agree with him that gruels and farinaceous articles are advisable during intermissions, when the patient craves for port, essence of beef, and consommé; nor can we readily admit the dictum that in the tropics "the most wholesome diet, without doubt, is chiefly vegetable." Despite Jacquemont and all the rice-eaters, I cry beef and beer for ever and everywhere! Many can testify personally to the value of the unofficinal prescription which he offers in cases of severe lichen (prickly heat), leading to impetigo. It is as follows, and it is valuable:—

Cold cream . . . ℥j.
Glycerine . . . . ʒj.
Chloroform . . . ʒij.
Oil of bitter almonds . . gtt. x.

CHAPTER IV.

THE MINOR TRIBES AND THE MPONGWE.

HE tribes occupying the Gaboon country may roughly be divided into two according to habitat—the maritime and those of the interior, who are *quasi*-mountaineers. Upon the sea-board dwell the Banôkô (Banaka), Bapuka, and Batanga; the Kombe, the Benga and Mbiko, or people about Corisco; the Shekyani, who extend far into the interior, the Urungu and Aloa, clans of Cape Lopez; the Nkommi, Commi, Camma or Cama, and the Mayumba races beyond the southern frontier. The inner hordes are the Dibwe (M. du Chaillu's "Ibouay"), the Mbúsha; the numerous and once powerful Bákele, the Cannibal Fá*n* (Mpongwe), the Osheba or 'Sheba, their congeners, and a variety of "bush-folk," of whom little is known beyond the names. Linguistically we may distribute them into three, namely, 1. the Banôkô and Batanga; 2. the Mpongwe, including the minor ethnical divisions of Benga, and Shekyani; the Urungu, the Nkommi, the Dongas or Ndiva, and the Mbúsha, and 3. the Mpongwe and the tribes of the interior. Lastly, there are only three peoples of any importance, namely, the Mpongwe, the Bákele, and the Fá*n*.

The Mpongwe, whom the French call "les Gabons," are the aristocracy of the coast, the Benga being the second, and the Banôkô and Bapuka ranking third. They are variously estimated at 5,000 to 7,000 head, serviles included. They inhabit both sides of the Gaboon, extending about thirty-five miles along its banks, chiefly on the right; on the left only seawards of the Shekyani. But it is a wandering race, and many a "mercator vagus" finds his way to Corisco, Cape Lopez, Batanga, and even Fernando Po. The two great families on the northern river bank are the Quabens and the Glass, who style themselves kings and princes; the southern side lodges King William (Roi Denis) near the mouth, and the powerful King George, about twenty-five miles higher up stream. There are also settlements scattered at various distances from the great highway of commerce to which they naturally cling, and upon the Coniquet and Parrot Islands.

Barbot (iv. 9) describes the "Gaboon blacks" as "commonly tall, robust, and well-shaped;" they appeared to me rather below the average of

West Coast size and weight. Both sexes, even when running to polysarcia, have delicate limbs and extremities, and the features, though negroid, are not the negro of the tobacconist's shop : I noticed several pyramidal and brachycephalic heads, contrary to the rule for African man and simiad. In the remarkable paper read (1861) by Professor Busk before the Ethnological Society, that eminent physiologist proved that the Asiatic apes, typified by the ourang-outang, are brachycephalic, like the Mongolians amongst whom they live, or who live amongst them; whilst the gorillas and the African anthropoids are dolichocephalic as the negroes. The Gaboon men are often almost black, whilst the women range between dark brown and *café au lait*. The beard, usually scanty, is sometimes *bien fournie*, especially amongst the seniors, but, whenever I saw a light-coloured and well-bearded man, the suspicion of mixed blood invariably obtruded itself. It is said that during the last thirty years they have greatly diminished, yet their habitat is still that laid down half a century ago by Bowdich, and all admit that the population of the river has not been materially affected.

The Mpongwe women have the reputation of being the prettiest and the most facile upon the West African coast. It is easy to distinguish two types. One is large-boned and heavy-limbed, hoarse-voiced, and masculine, like the "Ibos" of

Bonny and New Calabar, who equal the men in weight and stature, strength and endurance, suggesting a mixture of the male and female temperaments. Some of the Gaboon giantesses have,

THE PRETTY GABOON WOMAN.

unlike their northern sisters, regular and handsome features. The other type is *quasi*-Hindú in its delicacy of form, with small heads, oval faces, noses *à la Roxolane*, lips sub-tumid but without prognathism, and fine almond-shaped eyes, with remarkably thick and silky lashes. The throat is thin, the bosom is high and well carried, or, as the admiring Arab says, "nejdá;" the limbs are statuesque, and the hands and feet are Norman rather than Saxon. Many Europeans greatly admire these *minois mutins et chiffonés.*[1]

Early in the present century the Mpongwe braided whiskers and side curls, tipping the ends with small beads, and they plaited the front locks to project like horns, after the fashion of the present Fá*n* and other wild tribes. A custom noticed by Barbot, but apparently obsolete in the days of Bowdich, was to bore the upper lip, and to insert a small ivory pin, extending from nose to mouth. The painting and tattooing were fantastic and elaborate; and there was a hideous habit of splitting either lip, so as to "thrust the tongue through on ceremonial occasions." A curious reason is given for this practice. "They are subject to a certain distemper very common there, which on a sudden seizes them, and casts them into fits of so long a continuance, that they would inevitably be suffocated, if by means of the split at their upper lip they did not pour into their mouths some of the juice of a certain medicinal herb, which has the virtue of easing and curing the diseased person in a very short time."

[1] M. du Chaillu ends his chapter i. with an "illustration of a Mpongwe woman," copied without acknowledgment from Mr. Wilson's "Portrait of Yanawaz, a Gaboon Princess."

All these things, fits included, are now obsolete. The men shave a line in the hair like a fillet round the skull, and what is left is *coiffé au coup de vent.* The head-dress is a cap, a straw hat, a billy cock, or a tall silk "chimney pot," the latter denoting a chief; he also sports in full dress a broad coat, ending in a loin cloth of satin stripe or some finer stuff, about six feet long by four and a half broad; it is secured by a kerchief or an elastic waist belt; during work it is tucked up, but on ceremonial occasions it must trail upon the ground. The lieges wear European shirts, stuffed into a waist-cloth of cheaper material, calico or domestics; This Tángá, or kilt, is, in fact, an article of general wear, and it would be an airy, comfortable, and wholesome travelling costume if the material were flannel. The ornaments are necklaces of Venetian beads, the white pound, and the black and yellow seed: *Canutille* or bugles of various patterns are preferred, and all are loaded with "Mengo," Grígrís (which old travellers call "gregories"), or talismans, chiefly leopards' teeth, rude bells, and horns. The Monda are hunting prophylacteries, antelope horns filled with "fetish" medicines, leopard's hair, burnt and powdered heart mixed with leaves, and filth; the mouths are stopped with some viscid black stuff, probably gum. They are often attached to rude bells of iron or brass (Ige-lenga, Ngenge, Nkendo, or Wonga), like the

Chingufu of the Congo regions and the metal cones which are struck for signals upon the Tanganyika Lake.

A great man is known by his making himself a marvellous "guy," wearing, for instance, a dingily laced cocked hat, stuck athwart-ships upon an unwashed night-cap, and a naval or military uniform, fifty years old, "swearing" with the loin-cloth and the feet, which are always bare.

The coiffure of the ζῶον φιλόκοσμον is peculiar and elaborate as that of the Gold Coast. These ladies seem to have chosen for their model the touraco or cockatoo,—they have never heard of "Kikeriki,"—and the effect is at first wondrously grotesque. Presently the eye learns to admire pretty Fanny's ways; perhaps the *pleureuse*, the old English corkscrew ringlet, might strike the stranger as equally natural in a spaniel, and unnatural in a human. Still a style so peculiar requires a toilette in keeping; the "king" in uniform is less ridiculous than the Gaboon lady's chignon, contrasting with a tight-bodied and narrow-skirted gown of pink calico.

The national "tire-valiant" is a galeated crest not unlike the cuirassier's helmet, and the hair, trained from the sides into a high ridge running along the cranium, not unfrequently projects far beyond the forehead. Taste and caprice produce endless modifications. Sometimes the crest is double, disposed in parallel ridges, with a deep hollow between; or it is treble, when the two lines of parting running along the mastoids make it remarkably like bears' ears, the central prism rises high, and the side hair is plaited into little pig-tails. Others again train four parallel lines from nape to forehead, forming two cushions along the parietals. The crest is heightened by padding, and the whole of the hair is devoted to magnifying it,—at a distance, some of the bushwomen look as if they wore cocked hats. When dreaded baldness appears, rosettes of false hair patch the temples, and plaits of purchased wigs are interwoven to increase the bulk: the last resources of all are wigs and toupets of stained pine-apple fibre. The comb is unknown, its *succedaneum* being a huge bodkin, like that which the Trasteverina has so often used as a stiletto. This instrument of *castigation* is made of ivory or metal, with a lozenge often neatly carved and ornamented at the handle. The hair, always somewhat "kinky," is anointed every morning with palm-oil, or the tallow-like produce of a jungle-nut; and, in full dress, it is copiously powdered with light red or bright yellow dust of pounded camwood, redwood, and various barks.

The ears are adorned with broad rings of native make, and, near the trading stations, with French imitation jewellery. The neck supports many strings of beads, long and short, with the indispensable talismans. The body dress is a Tobe or loin-cloth, like that of the men; but under the "Námbá," or outer wrapper, which hangs down the feet, there is a "Siri," or petticoat, reaching only to the knees. Both are gathered in front like the Shukkah of the eastern coast, and the bosom is left bare. Few except the bush-folk now wear the Ibongo, Ipepe, or Ndengi, the woven fibres and grass-cloths of their ancestry; amongst the hunters, however, a Tángá, or grass-kilt, may still be seen. The exposure of the upper person shows the size and tumidity of the areola, even in young girls; being unsupported, the mammæ soon become flaccid.

The legs, which are peculiarly neat and well turned, are made by art a fitting set-off to the head. It is the pride of a Mpongwe wife to cover the lower limb between knee and ankle with an armour of metal rings, which are also worn upon the wrists; the custom is not modern, and travellers of the seventeenth century allude to them. The rich affect copper, bought in wires two feet and a half long, and in two sizes; of the larger, four, of the smaller, eight, go to the dollar; the brass are cheaper, as 5 : 4; and I did not see iron or tin. The native smiths make the circles, and the weight of a full set of forty varies from fifteen to nineteen pounds. They are separate rings, not a single coil, like that used by the Wagogo and other East African tribes; they press tightly on the limb, often causing painful chafes and sores. The ankle is generally occupied by a brass or iron chain, with small links. Girls may wear these rings, of which the husband is expected to present a considerable number to his bride, and the consequence is, that when in full dress she waddles like a duck.

Commerce and intercourse with whites has made the Mpongwe, once the rudest, now one of the most civilized of African tribes; and, upon the whole, there is an improvement. The exact Barbot (iv. 9) tells us "the Gaboon blacks are barbarous, wild, bloody, and treacherous, very thievish and crafty, especially towards strangers. The women, on the contrary, are as civil and courteous to them, and will use all possible means to enjoy their company; but both sexes are the most wretchedly poor and miserable of any in Guinea, and yet so very haughty, that they are perfectly ridiculous . . . They are all excessively fond of brandy and other strong liquors of Europe and America . . . If they fancy one has got a mouthful more than another, and they are half drunk, they will soon fall a-fighting, even with their own princes or priests . . . Their exceeding greediness for strong liquors renders them so little nice and curious in the choice of them, that, though mixed with half water, and sometimes a little Spanish soap put into it to give it a froth, to appear of proof by the scum it makes, they like it and praise it as much as the best and purest brandy." Captain Boteler remarks, in 1827: "The women do not speak English; though, for the sake of what trifles they can procure for their husbands, they are in the habit of flocking on board the different vessels which visit the river, and will permit them to remain; and the wives are generally maintained in clothing by the proceeds of their intercourse with the whites." He further assures us, that mulatto girls thus born are not allowed to marry, although there is no such restriction for the males; and elsewhere, he concludes, that never having seen an infant or an adult offspring of mixed blood, abortion is practised as at Delagoa and Old Calabar, where, in 1862, I found only one child of mixed blood. If so, the Mpongwe have changed for the better. Half-castes are now not uncommon; there are several nice "yaller gals" well known on the river; and the number of old and sick speaks well for the humanity of the tribe.

Devoted to trade and become a people of brokers, of go-betweens, of middle-men, the Mpongwe have now acquired an ease and propriety, a polish and urbanity of manner which contrasts strongly with the Kru-men and other tribes, who, despite generations of intercourse with Europeans, are rough and barbarous as their forefathers. The youths used to learn English, which they spoke fluently and with tolerable accent, but always barbarously; they are more successful with the easier neo-Latin tongues. Their one aim in life is not happiness, but "trust," an African practice unwisely encouraged by Europeans; so Old Calabar but a few years ago was not a trust-river," and consequently the consul and the gunboat had little to do there. Many of them have received advances of dollars by thousands, but the European merchant has generally suffered from his credulity or rapacity. In low cunning the native is more than a match for the stranger; moreover, he has "the pull" in the all-important matter of time; he can spend a fortnight haggling over the price of a tooth when the unhappy capitalist is eating his heart. Like all the African aristocracy, they hold agriculture beneath the dignity of man and fit only for their women and slaves; the "ladies" also refuse to work at the plantations, especially when young and pretty, leaving them to the bush-folk, male and female. M. du Chaillu repeatedly asserts (chap xix.) "there is no property in land," but this is a mistake often made in Africa. Labourers are hired at the rate of two to three dollars per mensem, and gangs would easily be collected if one of the chiefs were placed in command. No sum of money will buy a free-born Mpongwe, and the sale is forbidden by the laws of the land. A half-caste would fetch one hundred dollars; a wild "nigger" near the river costs from thirty to thirty-five dollars; the same may be bought in the Apinji country for four dollars' worth of assorted goods, the "bundle-trade" as it is called; but there is the imminent risk of the chattel's running away. A man's only attendants being now his wives and serviles, it is evident that plurality and domestic servitude will extend—

"Far into summers which we shall not see;"

in fact, till some violent revolution of society shall have introduced a servant class.

The three grades of Mpongwe may be considered as rude beginnings of caste. The first are the "Sons of the Soil," the "Ongwá ntye" (contracted from Onwana wi ntye), Mpongwes of pure blood; the second are the "Mbámbá," children of free-men by serviles; and lastly, "Nshákthree," in Bákele "Nshákă," represents the slaves. M. du Chaillu's distribution (chap. iii.) into five orders, namely, pure, mixed with other tribes, half free, children of serviles, and chattels, is somewhat over-artificial; at any rate, now it is not generally recognized. Like the high-caste Hindu, the nobler race will marry women of lower classes; for instance, King Njogoni's mother was a Benga; but the inverse proceeding is a disgrace to the woman, apparently an instinctive feeling on the part of the reproducer, still lingering in the most advanced societies. Old travellers record a belief that, unlike all other Guinea races, the Mpongwe marries his mother, sister, or daughter; and they compare the practice with that of the polished Persians and the Peruvian Incas, who thus kept pure the solar and lunar blood. If this "breeding-in" ever existed, no trace of it now remains; on the contrary, every care is taken to avoid marriages of consanguinity. Bowdich, indeed, assures us that a man may not look at nor converse with his mother-in-law, on pain of a heavy, perhaps a ruinous fine; "this singular law is founded on the tradition of an incest."

Marriage amongst the Mpongwe is a purely civil contract, as in Africa generally, and so perhaps it will some day be in Europe, Asia, and America. Cœlebs pays a certain sum for the bride, who, where "marriage by capture" is unknown, has no voice in the matter. Many promises of future "dash" are made to the girl's parents; and drinking, drumming, and dancing form the ceremony. The following is, or rather I should say was, a fair list of articles paid for a virgin bride. One fine silk hat, one cap, one coat; five to twenty pieces of various cottons, plain and ornamental; two to twenty silk kerchiefs; three to thirty jars of rum; twenty pounds of trade tobacco; two hatchets; two cutlasses; plates and dishes, mugs and glasses, five each; six knives; one kettle; one brass pan;

two to three Neptunes (caldrons, the old term being "Neptune's pots"), a dozen bars of iron; copper and brass rings, chains with small links, and minor articles *ad libitum*. The "settlement" is the same in kind, but has increased during the last forty years, and specie has become much more common.[1]

After marriage there is a mutual accommodation system suggesting the cicisbeo or *mariage à trois* school; hence we read that wives, like the much-maligned Xantippe, were borrowed and lent, and that not fulfilling the promise of a loan is punishable by heavy damages. Where the husband acts adjutor or *cavaliere* to his friend's "Omantwe"—female person or wife—and the friend is equally complaisant, wedlock may hardly be called permanent, and there can be no tie save children. The old immorality endures; it is as if the command were reversed by accepting that misprint which so scandalized the Star Chamber, "Thou shalt commit adultery." Yet, unpermitted, the offence is one against property, and Mœchus may be cast in damages ranging from $100 to $200: what is known in low civilization as the "panel dodge" is an infamy familiar to almost all the

[1] Everywhere on the lower river "hard dollars" are highly valued. The Spanish, formerly the favourite, and always worth 4*s*. 2*d*., command only a five-franc piece at Le Plateau; moreover, the "peseta," like the shilling, is taken as a franc.

maritime tribes of Africa. He must indeed be a Solomon of a son who, *sur les bords du Gabon*, can guess at his own sire; a question so impertinent is never put by the *ex-officio* father. The son succeeds by inheritance to his father's relict, who, being generally in years, is condemned to be useful when she has ceased to be an ornament, and, if there are several, they are equally divided amongst the heirs.

Trading tribes rarely affect the *pundonor* which characterizes the pastoral and the predatory; these people traffic in all things, even in the chastity of their women. What with pre-nuptial excesses, with early unions, often infructuous, with a virtual system of community, and with universal drunkenness, it is not to be wondered at if the maritime tribes of Africa degenerate and die out. Such apparently is the *modus operandi* by which Nature rids herself of the effete races which have served to clear the ground and to pave the way for higher successors. Wealth and luxury, so generally inveighed against by poets and divines, injure humanity only when they injuriously affect reproduction; and poverty is praised only because it breeds more men. The true tests of the physical prosperity of a race, and of its position in the world, are bodily strength and the excess of births over deaths.

Separation after marriage can hardly be dignified on the Gaboon by the name of divorce. Whenever a woman has or fancies she has a grievance, she leaves her husband, returns to "the paternal" and marries again. Quarrels about the sex are very common, yet, in cases of adultery the old murderous assaults are now rare except amongst the backwoodsmen. The habit was simply to shoot some man belonging to the seducer's or to the ravisher's village; the latter shot somebody in the nearest settlement, and so on till the affair was decided. In these days "violent retaliation for personal jealousy always 'be-littles' a man in the eyes of an African community." Perhaps also he unconsciously recognizes the sentiment ascribed to Mohammed, "Laysa bi-zányatin illa bi záni," "there is no adulteress without an adulterer," meaning that the husband has set the example.

Polygamy is, of course, the order of the day; it is a necessity to the men, and even the women disdain to marry a "one-wifer." As amongst all pluralists, from Moslem to Mormon, the senior or first married is No. 1; here called "best wife:" she is the goodman's viceroy, and she rules the home-kingdom with absolute sway. Yet the Mpongwe do not, like other tribes on the west coast, practise that separation of the sexes during gestation and lactation, which is enjoined to the Hebrews, recommended by Catholicism, and commanded by Mormonism—a system which partly justifies polygamy. In Portuguese Guinea the *enceinte* is claimed by her relatives, especially by the women, for three years, that she may give undivided attention to her offspring, who is rightly believed to be benefited by the separation, and that she may return to her husband with renewed vigour. Meanwhile custom allows the man to cohabit with a slave girl.

Polygamy, also, in Africa is rather a political than a domestic or social institution. A "judicious culture of the marriage tie" is necessary amongst savages and barbarians whose only friends and supporters are blood relations and nuptial connections; besides which, a multitude of wives ministers to the great man's pride and influence, as well as to his pleasures and to his efficiency. When the head wife ages, she takes charge of the girlish brides committed to her guardianship by the husband. I should try vainly to persuade the English woman that there can be peace in households so constituted: still, such is the case. Messrs. Wilson and Du Chaillu both assert that the wives rarely disagree amongst themselves. The sentimental part of love is modified; the common husband becomes the patriarch, not the paterfamilias; the wife is not the mistress, but the *mère de famille.* The alliance rises or sinks to one of interest and affection instead of being amorous or uxorious, whilst the underlying idea, "the more the merrier," especially in lands where free service is unknown, seems to stifle envy and jealousy. Everywhere, moreover, amongst polygamists, the husband is strictly forbidden by popular opinion to show preference for a favourite wife; if he do so, he is a bad man.

But polygamy here has not rendered the women, as theoretically it should, a down-trodden moiety of society; on the contrary, their position is comparatively high. The marriage connection is not "one of master and slave," a link between freedom and serfdom; the "weaker vessel" does not suffer from collision with the *pot de fer;* generally the fair but frail ones appear to be, as amongst the Israelites generally, the better halves. Despite the Okosunguu or cow-hide "peacemaker," they have conquered a considerable latitude of conducting their own affairs. When poor and slaveless and, naturally, when no longer young, they must work in the house and in the field, but this lot is not singular; in journeys they carry the load, yet it is rarely heavier than the weapons borne by the man. On the other hand, after feeding their husbands, what remains out of the fruits of their labours is their own, wholly out of his reach—a boon not always granted by civilization. As in Unyamwezi, they guard their rights with a truly feminine touchiness and jealousy. There is always, in the

African mind, a preference for descent and inheritance through the mother, "the surer side,"—an unmistakable sign, by the by, of barbarism. The so-called royal races in the eight great despotisms of Pagan Africa—Ashanti, Dahome, and Benin; Karagwah, Uganda, and Unyoro; the Mwátá yá Nvo, and the Mwátá Cazembe—allow the greatest liberty even to the king's sisters; they are expected only to choose handsome lovers, that the race may maintain its physical superiority; and hence, doubtless, the stalwart forms and the good looks remarked by every traveller. As a rule, the husband cannot sell his wife's children whilst her brother may dispose of them as he pleases—the *vox populi* exclaims, "What! is the man to go hungry when he can trade off his sister's brats?"

The strong-minded of London and New York have not yet succeeded in thoroughly organizing and popularizing their clubs; the *belles sauvages* of the Gaboon have. There is a secret order, called "Njembe," a Rights of Woman Association, intended mainly to counterbalance the Ndá of the lords of creation; which will presently be described. Dropped a few years ago by the men, it was taken up by their wives, and it now numbers a host of initiated, limited only by heavy entrance fees. This form of freemasonry deals largely in processions, whose preliminaries and proceedings are kept profoundly secret. At certain times an old woman strikes a stick upon an "Orega" or crescent-shaped drum, hollowed out of a block of wood; hearing this signal, the worshipful sisterhood, bedaubed, by way of insignia, with red and white chalk or clay, follow her from the village to some remote nook in the jungle, where the lodge is tiled. Sentinels are stationed around whilst business is transacted before a vestal fire, which must burn for a fortnight or three weeks, in the awe-compelling presence of a brass pipkin filled with herbs, and a basin, both zebra'd like the human limbs. The Rev. William Walker was once detected playing "Peeping Tom" by sixty or seventy viragos, who attempted to exact a fine of forty dollars, and who would have handled him severely had he not managed to escape. The French officers, never standing upon ceremony in such matters, have often insisted upon being present.

Circumcision, between the fourth and eighth year, is universal in Pongo-land, and without it a youth could not be married. The operation is performed generally by the chief, often by some old man, who receives a fee from the parents: the thumb nails are long, and are used after the Jewish fashion:[1] neat rum with red pepper is spirted

---

[1] "The British Jews," by the Rev. John Mills. London: Houlston and Stoneman, 1853.

from the mouth to "kill wound." It is purely hygienic, and not balanced by the *excisio Judaica*. Some physiologists consider the latter a necessary complement of the male rite; such, however, is not the case. The Hebrews, who almost everywhere retained circumcision, have, in Europe at least, long abandoned excision. I regret that the delicacy of the age does not allow me to be more explicit.

The Mpongwe practise a rite so resembling infant baptism that the missionaries have derived it from a corruption of Abyssinian Christianity which, like the flora of the Camarones and Fernandian Highlands, might have travelled across the Dark Continent, where it has now been superseded by El Islam. I purpose at some period of more leisure to prove an ancient intercourse and *rapprochement* of all the African tribes ranging between the parallels of north latitude 20° and south latitude 30°. It will best be established, not by the single great family of language, but by the similarity of manners, customs, and belief; of arts and crafts; of utensils and industry. The baptism of Pongo-land is as follows. When the babe is born, a crier, announcing the event, promises to it in the people's name participation in the rights of the living. It is placed upon a banana leaf, for which reason the plantain is never used to stop the waterpots; and the chief or the nearest of kin sprinkles it from a basin, gives it a name, and pronounces a benediction, his example being followed by all present. The man-child is exhorted to be truthful, and the girl to "tell plenty lie," in order to lead a happy life. Truly a new form of the regenerative rite!

A curious prepossession of the African mind, curious and yet general, in a land where population is the one want, and where issue is held the greatest blessing, is the imaginary necessity of limiting the family. Perhaps this form of infanticide is a policy derived from ancestors who found it necessary. In the kingdom of Apollonia (Guinea) the tenth child was always buried alive; never a *Decimus* was allowed to stand in the way of the nine seniors. The birth of twins is an evil portent to the Mpongwes, as it is in many parts of Central Africa, and even in the New World; it also involves the idea of moral turpitude, as if the woman were one of the lower animals, capable of superfetation. There is no greater insult to a man, than to point at him with two fingers, meaning that he is a twin; of course he is not one, or he would have been killed at birth. Albinos are allowed to live, as in Dahome, in Ashanti, and among some East African tribes, where I have been "chaffed" about a brother white, who proved to be an exceptional negro without *pigmentum nigrum*.

There is no novelty in the Mpongwe funeral rites; the same system prevails from the Oil Rivers to Congo-land, and extends even to the wild races of the interior. The corpse, being still sentient, is accompanied by stores of raiment, pots, and goats' flesh; a bottle is placed in one hand and a glass in the other, and, if the deceased has been fond of play, his draught-board and other materials are buried with him. The system has been well defined as one in which the "ghost of a man eats the ghost of a yam, boiled in the ghost of a pot, over the ghost of a fire." The body, after being stretched out in a box, is carried to a lonely place; some are buried deep, others close to the surface. There is an immense show of grief, with keening and crocodiles' tears, perhaps to benefit the living by averting a charge of witchcraft, which would inevitably lead to "Sassy" or poison-water. The wake continues for five days, when they "pull the cry," that is to say, end mourning. If these pious rites be neglected, the children incur the terrible reproach, "Your father he be hungry." The widow may re-marry immediately after "living for cry," and, if young and lusty, she looks out for another consort within the week. The slave is thrown out into the bush—no one will take the trouble to dig a hole for him.

The industry of the Mpongwe is that of the

African generally; every man is a host in himself; he builds and furnishes his house, he makes his weapons and pipes, and he ignores division of labour, except in the smith and the carpenter; in the potter, who works without a wheel, and in the dyer, who knows barks, and who fixes his colours with clay. The men especially pride themselves upon canoe-making; the favourite wood is the buoyant Okumeh or bombax, that monarch of the African forest. I have seen a boat, 45 feet 10 inches by 5 feet 11 inches in beam, cut out of a single tree, with the Mpáno or little adze, a lineal descendant of the Silex implement, and I have heard of others measuring 70 feet. These craft easily carry 10 tons, and travel 200 to 300 miles, which, as Mr. Wilson remarks, would land them, under favourable circumstances, in South America. Captain Boteler found that the Mpongwe boat combined symmetry of form, strength, and solidity, with safeness and swiftness either in pulling or sailing. And of late years the people have succeeded in launching large and fast craft built after European models.

The favourite pleasures of the Mpongwe are gross and gorging "feeds," drinking and smoking. They recall to mind the old woman who told "Monk Lewis" that if a glass of gin were at one end of the table, and her immortal soul at the other, she would choose the gin. They soak with palm-wine every day; they indulge in rum and absinthe, and the wealthy affect so-called Cognac, with Champagne and Bordeaux, which, however, they pronounce to be "cold." I have seen Master Boro, a boy five years old, drain without winking a wineglassful of brandy. It is not wonderful that the adults can "stand" but little, and that a few mouthfuls of well-watered spirit make their voices thick, and paralyze their weak brains as well as their tongues. The Persians, who commence drinking late in life, can swallow strong waters by the tumbler.

Men, women, and children when hardly "cremnobatic," have always the pipe in mouth. The favourite article is a "dudheen," a well *culotté* clay, used and worn till the bowl touches the nose. The poor are driven to a "Kondukwe," a yard of plantain leaf, hollowed with a wire, and charged at the thicker end. The "holy herb" would of course grow in the country, and grow well, but it is imported from the States without trouble, and perhaps with less expense. Some tribes make a decent snuff of the common trade article, but I never saw either sex chew—perhaps the most wholesome, and certainly the most efficacious form. The smoking of Lyámbá, called Dyámbá in the southern regions, is confined to debauchees. M. du Chaillu asserts that this *Cannabis sativa* is not found wild, and the people confirm his statement; possibly it has extended from Hindostan to Zanzibar, and thence across the continent. Intoxicating hemp is now grown everywhere, especially in the Nkommi country, and little packages, neatly bound with banana leaves, sell on the river for ten sous each. It is smoked either in the "Kondukwe" or in the Ojo. The latter, literally meaning a torch, is a polished cow-horn, closed at the thick end with wood, and banded with metal; a wooden stem, projecting from the upper or concave side, bears a neat "chillam" (bowl), either of clay or of brown steatite brought from the upper Gaboon River. This rude hookah is half filled with water; the dried hemp in the bowl is covered with what Syrians call a "Kurs," a bit of metal about the size of half-a-crown, and upon it rests the fire. I at once recognized the implement in the Brazil, where many slave-holders simply supposed it to be a servile and African form of tobacco-pipe. After a few puffs the eyes redden, a violent cough is caused by the acrid fumes tickling the throat; the brain, whirls with a pleasant swimming, like that of chloroform, and the smoker finds himself *in gloriâ*. My Spanish friends at Po tried but did not like it. I can answer for the hemp being stronger than the Egyptian hashísh or the bhang of Hindostan; it rather resembled the Fasúkh of Northern Africa, the Dakha and Motukwáne of the southern regions, and the wild variety called in Sind "Bang i Jabalí."

The religion of African races is ever interesting to those of a maturer faith; it is somewhat like the study of childhood to an old man. The Jew, the high-caste Hindú, and the Guebre, the Christian and the Moslem have their Holy Writs, their fixed forms of thought and worship, in fact their grooves in which belief runs. They no longer

THE WATER-PIPE.

see through a glass darkly; nothing with them is left vague or undetermined. Continuation, resurrection, eternity are hereditary and habitual ideas; they have become almost inseparable and congenital parts of the mental system. This condition renders it nearly as difficult for us to understand the vagueness and mistiness of savage and unwritten creeds, as to penetrate into the *modus agendi* of animal instinct. And there is yet another obstacle in dealing with such people, their intense and childish sensitiveness and secretiveness. They are not, as some have foolishly supposed, ashamed of their tenets or their practices, but they are unwilling to speak about them. They fear the intentions of the cross-questioner, and they hold themselves safest behind a crooked answer. Moreover, every Mpongwe is his own "pontifex maximus," and the want, or rather the scarcity, of a regular priesthood must promote independence and discrepancy of belief.

Whilst noticing the Fetishism of the Gaboon I cannot help observing, by the way, how rapidly the civilization of the nineteenth century is redeveloping, together with the "Religion of Humanity" the old faith, not of Paganism, but of Cosmos, of Nature; how directly it is, in fact, going back to its older gods. The UNKNOWABLE of our day is the Brahm, the Akarana-Zaman, the Gaboon Anyambía, of which nothing can be predicated but an existence utterly unintelligible to the brain of man, a something free from the accidents of personality, of volition, of intelligence, of design, of providence; a something which cannot be addressed by veneration or worship; whose sole effects are subjective, that is, upon the worshipper, not upon the worshipped. Nothing also can be more illogical than the awe and respect claimed by Mr. Herbert Spencer for a being of which the very essence is that nothing can be known of it. And, as the idea grows, the several modes and forms of the UNKNOWABLE, the Hormuzd and Ahriman of the Dualist, those personifications of good and evil; the Brahma, Vishnu, and Shiva, creation, preservation, and destruction; the beginning, the middle, and the end of all things; the Triad, adored by all Triadists under some modification, as that of Osiris, Isis, and Horus, father, mother, and son, type of the family; or Jupiter, Neptune, and Pluto, the three great elements; these outward and visible expressions lose force and significance, making place for that Law of which they are the rude exponents. The marvellous spread of Spiritualism, whose god is the UNKNOWABLE, and whose prophet was Swedenborg, is but the polished form of the Mpongwe Ibambo and Ilogo; the beneficent phantasms have succeeded to the malevolent ghosts, the shadowy deities of man's childhood; as the God of Love formerly took the place of the God of Fear. The future of Spiritualism, which may be defined as "Hades with Progress," is making serious inroads upon the coarse belief, worthy of the barbarous and the middle ages, in an eternity of punishment, easily expressed by everlasting fire, and in ineffable joys, which no one has ever successfully expressed. The ghosts of our childhood have now become *bonâ fide* objective beings, who rap, raise tables, display fireworks, rain flowers, and brew tea. We explain by "levitation" the riding of the witch upon the broom-stick to the Sabbath; we can no longer refuse credence to

Canidia and all her spells. And the very vagueness of the modern faith serves to assimilate it the more to its most ancient forms, one of which we are studying upon the Gaboon River.

The missionary returning from Africa is often asked what is the religion of the people? If an exact man, he will answer, "I don't know." And how can he know when the people themselves, even the princes and priests, are ignorant of it? A missionary of twenty years' standing in West Africa, an able and conscientious student withal, assured me that during the early part of his career he had given much time to collecting and collating, under intelligent native superintendence, negro traditions and religion. He presently found that no two men thought alike upon any single subject: I need hardly say that he gave up in despair a work hopeless as psychology, the mere study of the individual.

Fetishism, I believe, is held by the orthodox to be a degradation of the pure and primitive "Adamical dispensation," even as the negro has been supposed to represent the accursed and degraded descendants of Ham and Canaan. I cannot but look upon it as the first dawn of a faith in things not seen. And it must be studied by casting off all our preconceived ideas. For instance, Africans believe, not in soul nor in spirit, but in ghost; when they called M. du

Chaillu a "Mbwiri," they meant that the white man had been bleached by the grave as Dante had been darkened by his visit below, and consequently he was a subject of fear and awe. They have a material, evanescent, intelligible future, not an immaterial, incomprehensible eternity; the ghost endures only for awhile and perishes like the memory of the little-great name. Hence the ignoble dread in East and West Africa of a death which leads to a shadowy world, and eventually to utter annihilation. Seeing nought beyond the present-future, there is no hope for them in the grave; they wail and sorrow with a burden of despair. "Ame-kwisha"—he is finished—is the East African's last word concerning kinsman and friend. "All is done for ever," sing the West Africans. Any allusion to loss of life turns their black skins blue; "Yes," they exclaim, "it is bad to die, to leave house and home, wife and children; no more to wear soft cloth, nor eat meat, nor "drink" tobacco, and rum." "Never speak of *that*," the moribund will exclaim with a shudder; such is the ever-present horror of their dreadful and dreary times of sickness, always aggravated by suspicions of witchcraft, the only cause which their imperfect knowledge of physics can assign to death—even Van Helmont asserted, "Deus non fecit mortem." The peoples, who, like those of Dahome, have a distinct future world, have borrowed it, I cannot help thinking, from Egypt. And when an African chief said in my presence to a Yahoo-like naval officer, "When so be I die, I come up for white man! When so be you die, you come up for monkey!" my suspicion is that he had distorted the doctrine of some missionary. Man would hardly have a future without a distinct priestly class whose interest it is to teach "another and a better,"—or a worse.

Certain missionaries in the Gaboon River have detected evidences of Judaism amongst the Mpongwe, which deserve notice but which hardly require detailed refutation. 1. Circumcision, even on the eighth day as amongst the Efik of the old Calabar River; but this is a familiar custom borrowed from Egypt by the Semites; it is done in a multitude of ways, which are limited only by necessity; the resemblance of the Mpongwe rite to that of the Jews, though remarkable, is purely accidental. 2. The division of tribes into separate families and frequently into the number twelve; but this again appears fortuitous; almost all the West African people have some such division, and they range upwards from three, as amongst the Kru-men, the Gallas, the Wakwafi, and the Wanyika.[1] 3. Exogamy or the rigid interdiction of marriage between clans

[1] For further details see "Zanzibar City, Island, and Coast," vol. ii. chap. iv.

and families nearly related; here again the Hindú and the Somal observe the custom rigidly, whilst the Jews and Arabs have ever taken to wife their first cousins. 4. Sacrifices with blood-sprinkling upon altars and door-posts; a superstition almost universal, found in Peru and Mexico as in Palestine, preserved in Ashanti and probably borrowed by the Hebrews from the African Egyptians. 5. The formal and ceremonial observance of new moons; but the Wanyamwezi and other tribes also hail the appearance of the lesser light, like the Moslems, who, when they sight the Hilal (crescent), ejaculate a short prayer for blessings throughout the month which it ushers in. 6. A specified time of mourning for the dead (common to all barbarians as to civilized races), during which their survivors wear soiled clothes (an instinctive sign of grief, as fine dresses are of joy), and shave their heads (doubtless done to make some difference from every-day times), accompanied with ceremonial purifications (what ancient people has not had some such whim?). 7. The system of Runda or forbidden meats; but every traveller has found this practice in South as in East Africa, and I noticed it among the Somal who, even when starving, will not touch fish nor fowl. Briefly, external resemblances and coincidences like these could be made to establish cousinhood between a cockney and a cockatoo; possibly such discovery of Judaism dates from the days about 1840, when men were mad to find the "Lost Tribes," as if they had not quite enough to do with the two which remain to them.

The Mpongwe and their neighbours have advanced a long step beyond their black brethren in Eastern Africa. No longer contented with mere Fetishes, the Egyptian charms in which the dreaded ghost "sits,"[1] meaning, is "bound," they have invented idols, a manifest advance toward that polytheism and pantheism which lead through a triad and duad of deities to monotheism, the finial of the spiritual edifice. In Eastern Africa I know but one people, the Wanyika near Mombasah, who have certain images called "Kisukas;" they declare that this great medicine, never shown to Europeans, came from the West, and Andrew Battel (1600) found idols amongst the people whom he calls Giagas or Jagas, meaning Congoese chiefs. Moreover, the Gaboon pagans lodge their idols. Behind each larger establishment there is a dwarf hut, the miniature of a dwelling-place, carefully closed; I thought these were offices, but Hotaloya Andrews taught me otherwise. He called them in his broken English "Compass-houses," a literal translation of "Nágo Mbwiri," and, sturdily refusing me admittance, left me as

[1] See "Zanzibar City, Island, and Coast," vol. ii. chap. v.

wise as before. The reason afterwards proved to be that "Ologo he kill man too much."

I presently found out that he called my pocket compass, "Mbwiri," a very vague and comprehensive word. It represents in the highest signification the Columbian Manitou, and thus men talk of the Mbwiri of a tree or a river; as will presently be seen, it is also applied to a tutelar god; and I have shown how it means a ghost. In "Nágo Mbwiri" the sense is an idol, an object of worship, a "medicine" as the North-American Indians say, in contradistinction to Munda, a grigri, talisman, or charm. Every Mpongwe, woman as well as man, has some Mbwiri to which offerings are made in times of misfortune, sickness, or danger. I afterwards managed to enter one of these rude and embryonal temples so carefully shut. Behind the little door of matting is a tall threshold of board; a bench lines the far end, and in the centre stands "Ologo," a rude imitation of a human figure, with a gum-torch planted in the ground before it ready for burnt offerings. To the walls are suspended sundry mystic implements, especially basins, smeared with red and white chalk-mixture, and wooden crescents decorated with beads and ribbons.

During worship certain objects are placed before the Joss, the suppliant at the same time jangling and shaking the Ncheke a rude beginning of the bell, the gong, the rattle, and the instruments played before idols by more advanced peoples. It is a piece of wood, hour-glass-shaped but flat, and some six inches and a half long; the girth of the waist is five inches, and about three more round the ends. The wood is cut away, leaving rude and uneven raised bands horizontally striped with white, black, and red. Two brass wires are stretched across the upper and lower breadth, and each is provided with a ring or hinge holding four or five strips of wire acting as clappers.

This "wicker-work rattle to drive the devil out" (M. du Chaillu, chap. xxvi.) is called by the Mpongwe "Soke," and serves only, like that of the Dahomans and the Ashantis (Bowdich, 364) for dancing and merriment. The South American Maracá was the sole object of worship known to the Tupi or Brazilian "Indians." [1]

The beliefs and superstitions popularly attributed to the Mpongwe are these. They are not without that which we call a First Cause, and they name it Anyambía, which missionary philologists consider a contraction of Aninla, spirit (?), and Mbia, good. M. du Chaillu everywhere confounds Anyam-

---

[1] See part ii. chap. xxii. "Hans Stade," translated by Mr. Albert Tootal, annotated by myself, and published by the Hakluyt Society, 1874.

bía, or, as he writes the word, "Aniambié," with Inyemba, a witch, to bewitch being "punga inyemba." Mr. W. Winwood Reade seems to make Anyambía a mysterious word, as was Jehovah after the date of the Moabite stone. Like the Brahm of the Hindus, the god of Epicurus and Confucius, and the Akárana-Zaman or Endless Time of the Guebres, Anyambía is a vague being, a *vox et præterea nihil*, without personality, too high and too remote for interference in human affairs, therefore not addressed in prayer, never represented by the human form, never lodged in temples. Under this "unknown God" are two chief agencies, working partners who manage the business of the world, and who effect what the civilized call "Providence." Mbwírí here becomes the Osiris, Jove, Hormuzd or Good God, the Vishnu, or Preserver, a tutelar deity, a Lar, a guardian. Onyámbe is the Bad God, Typhon, Vejovis, the Ahriman or Semitic devil; Shiva the Destroyer, the third person of the Aryan triad; and his name is never mentioned but with bated breath. They have not only fear of, but also a higher respect for him than for the giver of good, so difficult is it for the child-man's mind to connect the ideas of benignity and power. He would harm if he could, *ergo* so would his god. I once hesitated to believe that these rude people had arrived at the notion of duality, at the Manichæanism which caused Mr. Mill (sen.) surprise that no one had revived it in his time; at an idea so philosophical, which leads directly to the *ne plus ultra* of faith, El Wahdániyyeh or Monotheism. Nor should I have credited them with so logical an apparatus for the regimen of the universe, or so stout-hearted an attempt to solve the eternal riddle of good and evil. But the same belief also exists amongst the Congoese tribes, and even in the debased races of the Niger. Captain William Allen ("Niger Expedition," i. 227) thus records the effect when, at the request of the commissioners, Herr Schön, the missionary, began stating to King Obi the difference between the Christian religion and heathenism:

"*Herr Schön.* There is but one God.

"*King Obi.* I always understood there were two," &c.

The Mpongwe "Mwetye" is a branch of male freemasonry into which women and strangers are never initiated. The Bakele and Shekyani, according to "Western Africa" (Wilson, pp. 391-2), consider it a "Great Spirit." Nothing is more common amongst adjoining negro tribes than to annex one another's superstitions, completely changing, withal, their significance. "Ovengwá" is a vampire, the apparition of a dead man; tall as a tree, always winking and clearly seen, which is not the case with the Ibámbo and Ilogo, plurals of Obambo and

Ologo. These are vulgar ghosts of the departed, the causes of "possession," disease and death; they are propitiated by various rites, and everywhere they are worshipped in private. Mr. Wilson opines that the "Obambo are the spirits of the ancestors of the people, and Inlâgâ are the spirits of strangers and have come from a distance," but this was probably an individual tenet. The Mumbo-Jumbo of the Mandengas; the Semo of the Súsús; the Tassau or "Purrah-devil" of the Mendis; the Egugun of the Egbas; the Egbo of the Duallas; and the Mwetye and Ukukwe of the Bakele, is represented in Pongo-land by the Ndá, which is an order of the young men. Ndá dwells in the woods and comes forth only by night bundled up in dry plantain leaves[1] and treading on tall stilts; he precedes free adult males who parade the streets with dance and song. The women and children fly at the approach of this devil on two sticks, and with reason: every peccadillo is punished with a merciless thrashing. The institution is intended to keep in order the weaker sex, the young and the "chattels:" Ndá has tried visiting white men and missionaries, but his visits have not been a success.

---

[1] Captain Boteler (v. ii. p. 374) gives a sketch of the "Fetiche dance, Cape Lopez," and an admirable description of Ndá, who is mounted on stilts with a white mask, followed by negroes with chalked faces.

The civilized man would be apt to imagine that these wild African fetishists are easily converted to a "purer creed." The contrary is everywhere and absolutely the case; their faith is a web woven with threads of iron. The negro finds it almost impossible to rid himself of his belief; the spiritual despotism is the expression of his organization, a part of himself. Progressive races, on the other hand, can throw off or exchange every part of their religion, except perhaps the remnant of original and natural belief in things unseen—in fact, the Fetishist portion, such as ghost-existence and veneration of material objects, places, and things. I might instance the Protestant missionary who, while deriding the holy places at Jerusalem, considers the "Cedars of Lebanon" sacred things, and sternly forbids travellers to gather the cones.

The stereotyped African answer to Europeans ridiculing these institutions, including wizard-spearing and witch-burning is, "There *may* be no magic, though I see there is, among you whites. But we blacks have known many men who have been bewitched and died." Even in Asia, whenever I spoke contemptuously to a Moslem of his Jinns, or to a Hindu of his Rákshasa, the rejoinder invariably was, "You white men are by nature so hot that even our devils fear you."

Witchcraft, which has by no means thoroughly

disappeared from Europe, maintains firm hold upon the African brain. The idea is found amongst Christians, for instance, the "reduced Indians" of the Amazonas River; and it is evidently at the bottom of that widely spread superstition, the "evil eye," which remains throughout Southern Europe as strong as it was in the days of Pliny. As amongst barbarians generally, no misfortune happens, no accident occurs, no illness nor death can take place without the agency of wizard or witch. There is nothing more odious than this crime; it is hostile to God and man, and it must be expiated by death in the most terrible tortures. Metamorphosis is a common art amongst Mpongwe magicians: this vulgar materialism, of which Ovid sang, must not be confounded with the poetical Hindu metempsychosis or transmigration of souls which explains empirically certain physiological mysteries. Here the adept naturally becomes a gorilla or a leopard, as he would be a lion in South Africa, a hyena in Abyssinia and the Somali country, and a *loup-garou* in Brittany.[1]

The poison ordeal is a necessary corollary to witchcraft. The plant most used by the Oganga (medicine man) is a small red-rooted shrub, not unlike a hazel bush, and called Ikázyá or Ikájá. Mr. Wilson (p. 225) writes "Nkazya:" Battel (loc.

[1] See "Zanzibar, City, Island, and Coast," vol. i. chap. vii.

cit. 334) terms the root "Imbando," a corruption of Mbundú. M. du Chaillu (chap. xv.) gives an illustration of the "Mboundou leaf" (half size): Professor John Torrey believes the active principle to be a vegeto-alkali of the *Strychnos* group, but the symptoms do not seem to bear out the conjecture. The Mpongwe told me that the poison was named either Mbundú or Olondá (nut) werere—perhaps this was what is popularly called "a sell." Mbundú is the decoction of the scraped bark which corresponds with the "Sassy-water" of the northern maritime tribes. The accused, after drinking the potion, is ordered to step over sticks of the same plant, which are placed a pace apart. If the man be affected, he raises his foot like a horse with string-halt, and this convicts him of the foul crime. Of course there is some antidote, as the medicine-man himself drinks large draughts of his own stuff: in Old Calabar River for instance, Mithridates boils the poison-nut; but Europeans could not, and natives would not, tell me what the Gaboon "dodge" is. According to vulgar Africans, all test-poisons are sentient and reasoning beings, who search the criminal's stomach, that is his heart, and who find out the deep hidden sin; hence the people shout, "If they are wizards, let it kill them; if they are innocent, let it go forth!" Moreover, the detected murderer is considered a bungler who has fallen into the pit dug for his brother. Doubtless many innocent lives have been lost by this superstition. But there is reason in the order, "Thou shalt not suffer a witch to live," without having recourse to the supernaturalisms and preternaturalisms, which have unobligingly disappeared when Science most wants them. Sorcery and poison are as closely united as the "Black Nightingales," and it evidently differs little whether I slay a man with my sword or I destroy him by the slow and certain torture of a mind diseased.

The Mpongwe have also some peculiarities in their notions of justice. If a man murder another, the criminal is put to death, not by the nearest of kin, as amongst the Arabs and almost all wild people, but by the whole community; this already shows an advanced appreciation of the act and its bearings. The penalty is either drowning or burning alive: except in the case of a chief or a very rich man, little or no difference is made between wilful murder, justifiable homicide, and accidental manslaughter—the reason of this, say their jurists, is to make people more careful. Here, again, we find a sense of the sanctity of life the reverse of barbarous. Cutting and maiming are punished by the fine of a slave.

And now briefly to resume the character of the Mpongwe, a nervous and excitable race of negroes. The men are deficient in courage, as the women are in chastity, and neither sex has a tincture of what we call morality. To commercial shrewdness and eagerness they add exceptional greed of gain and rascality; foreign rum and tobacco, dress and ornaments, arms and ammunition have been necessaries to them; they *will* have them, and, unless they can supply themselves by licit, they naturally fly to illicit means. Yet, despite threats of poison and charges of witchcraft, they have arrived at an inkling of the dogma that "honesty is the best *policy*:" the East African has never dreamed it in the moments of his wildest imagination. Pre-eminent liars, they are, curious to say, often deceived by the falsehoods of others, and they fairly illustrate the somewhat paradoxical proverb:

> "He who hates truth shall be the dupe of lies."

Unblushing mendicants, cunning and calculating, their obstinacy is remarkable; yet, as we often find the African, they are at the same time irresolute in the extreme. Their virtues are vivacity, mental activity, acute observation, sociability, politeness, and hospitality: the fact that a white man can wander single-handed through the country shows a kindly nature. The brightest spot in their character is an abnormal development of adhesiveness, popularly called affection; it is somewhat tempered by capricious ruffianism, as in children; yet it entitles them to the gratitude of travellers.

The language of the Mpongwe has been fairly studied. T. Edward Bowdich ("Mission from Cape Coast Castle to Ashantee," London, Murray, 1819) when leaving the West Coast for England, touched at the Gaboon in a trading vessel, and visited Naango (King George's Town), on Abaaga Creek, which he places fifty miles up stream. He first gave (Appendix VI.) a list of the Mpongwe numerals. In 1847 the "Missionaries of the A. B. C. F. M." Gaboon Mission, Western Africa, printed a "Grammar of the Mpongwe Language, with Vocabularies" (New York, Snowden and Pratt, Vesey Street), perhaps a little prematurely; it is the first of the four dialects on this part of the coast reduced to system by the American Missionaries, especially by the Rev. Mr. Leighton Wilson, the others being Bakele, Benga, and Fá*n*.

In 1856, the same gentleman, who had taken the chief part in the first publication, made an able abstract and a comparison with the Grebo and Mandenga tongues ("Western Africa," part iv. chap. iv.). M. du Chaillu further abridged this abridgement in his Appendix without owning his authority, and in changing the examples he did all possible damage. In the Transactions of the Ethnological Society of London (part ii. vol. i. new series), he also gave an abstract, in which he repeats himself. A "*voca-*

bulaire de la langue Ponga" was printed in the "Mémoires de la Société Ethnologique," tome ii., by M. P. H. Delaporte.

The other publications known to me are :—

1. The Book of Proverbs, translated into the Mpongwe language at the mission of the A. B. C. F. M., Gaboon, West Africa. New York. American Bible Society, instituted in the year MDCCCXVI. 1859.

2. The Books of Genesis, part of Exodus, Proverbs, and Acts, by the same, printed at the same place and in the same year.

The missionary explorers of the language, if I may so call them, at once saw that it belongs to the great South African family Sichwáná, Zulu, Kisawahíli, Mbundo (Congoese), Fiote, and others, whose characteristics are polysyllabism, inflection by systematic prefixes, and an alliteration, the mystery of whose reciprocal letters is theoretically explained by a euphony in many cases unintelligible, like the modes of Hindú music, to the European ear.[1] But they naturally fell into the universally accepted error of asserting "it has no known affinities to any of the languages north of the Mountains of the Moon," meaning the equatorial chain which divides the Niger and Nile valleys from the basin of the Congo.

[1] I have discussed this subject in my "Zanzibar," vol. i. chap. xi.

This branch has its peculiarities. Like Italian—the coquette who grants her smiles to many, her favours to few—one of the easiest to understand and to speak a little, it is very difficult to master. Whilst every native child can thread its way safely through its intricate, elaborate, and apparently arbitrary variations, the people comprehend a stranger who blunders over every sentence. Mr. Wilson thus limits the use of the accent: "Whilst the Mandenga ("A Grammar of the Mandenga Language," by the Rev. R. Maxwell Macbriar, London, John Mason) and the Grebo ("Grammar," by the Right Rev. John Payne, D.D. 150, Nassau Street, New York, 1864), distinguish between similar words, especially monosyllables, by a certain pitch of voice, the Mpongwe repel accent, and rely solely upon the clear and distinct vowel sounds." But I found the negative past, present, and future forms of verbs wholly dependent upon a change of accent, or rather of intonation or voice-pitch, which the stranger's ear, unless acute, will fail to detect. For instance, *Mi Taundă* would mean "I love;" *Mi taundá*, "I do not love." The reverend linguist also asserts that it is almost entirely free from guttural and nasal sounds; the latter appeared to me as numerous and complicated as in the Sanskrit. Mr. Wilson could hardly have had a nice ear, or he would not have written Nchígo "Ntyege," or

Njína "Engena," which gives a thoroughly un-African distinctness to the initial consonant.

The adjectival form is archaically expressed by a second and abstract substantive. This peculiarity is common in the South African family, as in Ashanti; but, as Bowdich observes, we also find it in Greek, *e.g.* Αἱρέσεις ἀπωλείας, "heresies of destruction" for destructive. Another notable characteristic is the Mpongwe's fondness for the passive voice, never using, if possible, the active; for instance, instead of saying, "He was born thus," he prefers, "The birth that was thus borned by him." The dialect changes the final as well as the initial syllable, a process unknown to the purest types of the South African family. As we advance north we find this phenomenon ever increasing; for instance in Fernando Po; but the Mpongwe limits the change to verbs.

Another distinguishing point of these three Gaboon tongues, as the Rev. Mr. Mackey observes, is "the surprizing flexibility of the verb, the almost endless variety of parts regularly derived from a single root. There are, perhaps, no other languages in the world that approach them in the variety and extent of the inflections of the verb, possessing at the same time such rigid regularity of conjugation and precision of the meaning attached to each part." It is calculated that the whole number of tenses or shades of meaning which a Mpongwe radical verb may be made to express, with the aid of its auxiliary particles, augmentatives, and negatives—prefixes, infixes, and suffixes—is between twelve and fifteen hundred, worse than an Arabic triliteral.

Liquid and eminently harmonious, concise and capable of contraction, the Mpongwe tongue does not deserve to die out. "The genius of the language is such that new terms may be introduced in relation to ethics, metaphysics, and science; even to the great truths of the Christian religion."

The main defect is that of the South African languages generally—a deficiency of syntax, of gender and case; a want of vigour in sound; a too great precision of expression, rendering it clumsy and unwieldy; and an absence of exceptions, which give beauty and variety to speech. The people have never invented any form of alphabet, yet the abundance of tale, legend, and proverb which their dialect contains might repay the trouble of acquiring it.

CHAPTER V.

TO SÁNGA-TÁNGA AND BACK.

MY objects in visiting Mbátá, the reader will have understood, were to shoot a specimen or specimens of the gorilla, and, if possible, to buy or catch a youngster. Even before landing, the pilot had assured me that a "baby" was on sale at the Comptoir, but on inquiry it proved to have died. I was by no means sanguine of success—when the fight is against Time, the Old Man usually wins the day. The short limits of my trip would not allow me to wander beyond the coast and the nearer riverine regions, where frequent villages and the constant firing of muskets have taught all wild animals that flight is their only defence; thus, besides being rare, they must be shy and timid, wary and knowing, "like an old hedgehog hunted for his grease." The first glance at the bush suggested, "Surely it is impossible to find big game in such a land of farms and plantations."

Those who have shot under such circumstances will readily understand that everything depends upon "luck;" one man may beat the forest assiduously and vainly for five or six weeks; another will be successful on the first day. Thus whilst I, without any fault of my own, utterly failed in shooting a gorilla, although I saw him and heard him, and came upon his trail, and found his mortal spoils, another traveller had hardly landed in the Gaboon before he was so fortunate as to bring down a fine anthropoid.

However, as man cannot command success, I was obliged to content myself with doing all in my power to deserve it. I offered five dollars, equalling the same number of sovereigns in England, to every huntsman for every fair shot, and ten dollars for each live ape. I implicitly obeyed all words of command, and my factotum Selim Agha was indefatigable in his zeal. Indeed "luck" was dead against us during the whole of my stay in Gorilla-land. We ran a fair risk of drowning in the first day's voyage; on the next march we were knocked down by lightning, and on the last trip I had a narrow escape from the fall of a giant branch that grazed my hammock.

My first "bush" evening was spent in palm-wine, rum, and wassail; one must begin by humouring Africans, under pain of being considered a churl; but the inevitable result is, that next day they will by some pretext or other shirk work to enjoy the headache. That old villain, "Young Prince," becoming very *fou*, hospitably offered me his daughter-in-law Azízeh, Forteune's second wife; and he was vigorously supported by the Nimrod himself, who had drawn a horizontal line of white chalk above the eyebrows, a defence against the Ibambo, those bad ghosts that cause fevers and sickness. Forteune then hinted that perhaps I might prefer his daughter—"he be piccanniny; he be all same woman." *Marchandise offerte a le pied coupé*, both offers were declined with, *Merci, non!* Sporting parties are often made up by the Messieurs du Plateau, I had been told at the Comptoir; but such are the fascinations of *les petites*, that few ever progress beyond the first village. There was, consequently, wonder in the land as to what manner of utangáni this one might be.

It is only fair to own that the ladies endured with great philosophy the *spretæ injuria formæ*, and made no difference in their behaviour on account of their charms being unappreciated. Azízeh was a stout and sturdy personage of twenty-five, with thick wrists and ankles, a very dark skin, and a face rendered pleasing by good humour. And Azízeh was childless, a sad reproach in these lands, where progeny forms a man's wealth and a woman's honour.

The next day was perforce a halt, as had been expected; moreover, rains and tornadoes were a reasonable pretext for nursing the headache. The 21st was also wet and stormy, so Nimrod hid himself and was not to be found. Then the *balivernes* began. One Asini, a Mpongwe from the Plateau, offered to show me a huge gorilla near his village; in the afternoon he was confronted with "Young Prince," and he would have blushed scarlet if he could. But he assured me plaintively that he must lie to live, and, after all, *la prudence des souris n'est pas celle des chats.* Before dark, Forteune appeared, and swore that he had spent the day in the forest, he had shot at a gorilla, but the gun missed fire—of course he had slept in a snug hut.

This last determined me to leave Mbátá; the three Kru-men had returned; one of them was stationed in charge of the boat, and next morning we set out at 6 A.M. for Nche Mpolo, the head-quarters of "Young Prince." The well-wooded land was devoid of fetor, even at that early hour; we passed Ndagola, a fresh clearing and newly built huts, and then we skirted a deep and forested depression, upon whose further side lay our bourne. It promised sand-flies, the prime pest of this region; a tall amphitheatre of trees on a dune to the west excluded the sea-breeze, and northwards a swampy hollow was a fine breeding place for *M. Maringouin.*

Nche Mpolo lies some three miles nearly due south of Mbátá; the single street contains fourteen cottages and two palaver houses. We were received with distinction by "Young Prince's" daughter, a huge young woman, whose still huger mamma was from Cape Lopez. She placed mats upon the bamboo couch under the verandah, brought water to wash our feet, and put the kettle on that we might have tea. The sun was fiery and the day sultry; my companions complained of fatigue after a two hours' walk, and then busied themselves ostentatiously in cleaning their muskets, in collecting provisions, and in appointing certain bushmen to meet us on the morrow. Before dark Hotaloya returned to his village, declaring that he could find no bed at his papa's. Probably the uxorious youth had been ordered home by his pet wife, who had once lived with a European trader, who spoke a few words of English, and who cooked with peculiar skill,—the solid merits of a "superior person."

At dawn on the 23rd we set out for the southern bush, Selim, Forteune, and a carrier Kru-man—to carry nothing. We passed through a fresh clearing, we traversed another village (three within five miles!), we crossed a bad bridge and a clear stream flowing to the south-east, and presently we found ourselves deep in the dew-dripping forest. The leaves no longer crackled crisp under foot, and the late rains had made the swamps somewhat odorous. After an hour of cautious walking, listening as we went, we saw evident signs of Mister Gorilla. Boughs three inches in diameter strewed the ground; the husks of Ntondo or Ibere (wild cardamom) had been scattered about, and a huge hare's form of leaves lay some five yards from the tree where Forteune declared that Mistress and Master Gorilla had passed the night, Paterfamilias keeping watch below. A little beyond we were shown a spot where two males had been fighting a duel, or where a couple had been indulging in dalliance sweet; the prints were 8 inches long and 6 across the huge round toes; whilst the hinder hand appeared almost bifurcate, the thumb forming nearly a half. This is explained in the "Gorilla Book" (chap. xx.): "Only the ball of the foot, and that thumb which answers to our great toe, seem to touch the ground."

Presently we came upon the five bushmen who had been appointed to meet us. They were a queer-looking lot, with wild, unsteady eyes, receding brows, horizontal noses, and projecting muzzles; the cranium and the features seemed disposed nearly at a right angle, giving them a peculiar baboon-like semblance. Each had his water-gourd and his flint-gun, the lock protected by a cover of monkey's skin or wild cow's hide, whilst *gibecières* and ammunition-bags of grass-cloth hung from their shoulders. There were also two boys with native axes, small iron triangles, whose points passed through knob-sticks; these were to fell the trees in which our game might take refuge, and possibly they might have done so in a week. A few minutes with this party convinced me that I was wilfully wasting time; they would not separate, and they talked so loud that game would be startled a mile off. I proposed that they should station me in a likely place, form a circle, and drive up what was in it—they were far above acting beaters after that fashion. So we dismissed them and dispersed about the bush. My factotum shot a fine Mboko (*Siurus eborivorus*), 2 ft. 2 in. total length: the people declare that this squirrel gnaws ivory, whence its name. I had heard of it in East and Central Africa, but the tale appeared fabulous: here it is very common, half a dozen will be seen during the day; it has great vitality, and it will escape after severe wounds. The bushmen also brought a Shoke (*Colubus Satanas*), a small black monkey, remarkably large limbed: the little unfortunate was timid, but not vicious; it worried itself to death on the next day. They also showed me the head of the Njíwo antelope, which M. du Chaillu (chap. xii.) describes as "a singular animal of the size of a donkey, with shorter legs, no horns, and black, with a yellow spot on the back."

In the afternoon Selim went to fetch my arsenical soap from Mbátá, where I had left it *en Fitiché*: as long as that "bad medicine" was within Hotaloya's "ben," no one would dare to meddle with my goods. Forteune walked in very tired about sunset. He had now added streaks of red to the white chalk upon his face, arms, and breast, for he suspected, we were assured, witchcraft. I told him to get ready for a march on the morrow to the Shekyáni country, lying south-east, but he begged so hard, and he seemed so assured of showing sport, that the design was deferred, and again "perdidi diem."

Monday the 24th was a Black Monday, sultry and thundery. We went to the bush, and once more we returned, disgusted by the chattering of the wild men. As we discussed our plans for moving, Forteune threw cold water upon every proposal. This puzzled me, and the difficulty was to draw his secret. At last Kángá, a black youth, who, being one of the family, had attached himself uninvited to the party, blurted out in bad French that the Shekyáni chief, to whose settlement we were bound, had left for the interior, and that the

---

[1] M. du Chaillu's description of the animal is excellent (p. 282), and the people at once recognized the cut.

village women would not, or rather could not, give us "chop." This was a settler to my Mpongwe friends. Nimrod, however, declared that some bushmen had lately seen several gorillas in the direction of Sánga-Tánga, two marches down coast from Mbátá, and about half-way to Cape Lopez. I did not believe a word of his intelligence; the direction is south-west instead of south-east, towards the sea instead of into the forest. But it was evidently hopeless to seek for the "ole man" in these parts, and I had long been anxious to see Sánga-Tánga; we therefore agreed *nem. con.* to set out before dawn on the next day.

But the next day dawned, and the sun rose high, and the world was well heated and aired before the bushmen condescended to appear. After a two hours' battle with the sand-flies we set off at 7.35 A.M., Forteune, Hotaloya, and Kángá at the head of the musketeers, one of them also carrying an axe; sixteen guns form a strong party for these regions. The viol (nchámbí) was not allowed to hang mute in Mbátá's halls, this instrument or the drum must never be neglected in African travel; its melody at the halt and the camp-fire are to the negro what private theatricals are to the European sailor half fossilized in the frozen seas. Our specimen was strung with thin cords made from the fibre of a lliana; I was shown this growth, which looked much like a convolvulus.

The people have a long list of instruments, and their music, though monotonous, is soft and plaintive: Bowdich gives a specimen of it ("Sketch of Gaboon," p. 449), and of a bard who seems to have been somewhat more frenzied than most poets. Captain Allen (iii. 398) speaks of a harp at Bimbia (Camarones) tightly strung with the hard fibre of some creeping plant. The Bákele harp (M. du Chaillu, chap. xvi.) is called Ngombi; the handle opposite the bow often has a carved face, and it might be a

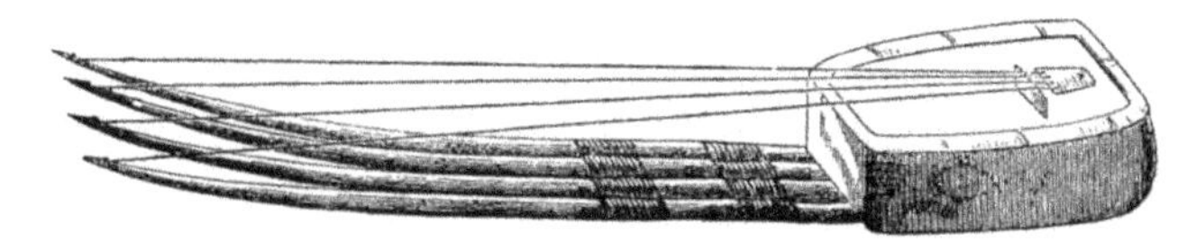

GABOON HARP.

beginning of the article used by civilized Europe —Wales for instance.

The path plunged westward into the bush, spanned a dirty and grass-grown plantation of bananas, dived under thorn tunnels and arches of bush, and crossed six nullahs, Neropotamoi, then dry, but full of water on our return. The ant-nests were those of Yoruba and the Mendi country; not the tall, steepled edifices built by the termites with yellow clay, as in Eastern Africa, but an eruption of blue-black, hard-dried mud and mucus, resembling the miniature pagodas, policeman's lanterns, mushrooms, or umbrellas one or two feet high, here single, there double, common in Ashanti and Congo-land. Like most of their *congeners*, the animals die when exposed to the sun. The "Bashikouay" and Nchounou (Nchu'u) of M. du Chaillu are the common "driver-ant" of West Africa (*Termes bellicosa*). It is little feared in the Gaboon; when its armies attack the mission-houses, they are easily stopped by lighting spirits of turpentine, or by a strew of quicklime, which combines with the formic acid. The different species are described in "Palm Land" and "Western Africa" (pp. 369-373), from which even the account of the "tubular bridge" is taken—Mr. Wilson less sensationally calls it what it is, a "live raft." The most common are the Nkázeze, a large reddish and fetid ant, which is harmless to man; the Njenge, a smaller red species, and the Ibimbízí, whose bite is painful.

We passed the mortal remains of a gorilla lashed to a pole; the most interesting parts had been sold to Mr. R. B. N. Walker, and were on their way to England. I was shown for the first time the Ndámbo, or Ndambié (Bowdich, "Olamboo"), which gives the india rubber of commerce; it is not a fat-leaved fig-tree (*Ficus elastica* of Asia) nor aeuphorbia (*Siphonia elastica*), as in South America, but a large climbing ficus, a cable thick as a man's leg crossing the path, and "swarming up" to the top of the tallest boles; the yellow fruit is tart and pleasant to the taste. In 1817 the style of collecting the gum (olamboo) was to spread with a knife the glutinous milk as it oozed from the tree over the shaved breast and arms like a plaister; it was then taken off, rolled up in balls to play with or stretched over drums, no other use being known. The Rev. Mr. Wilson declares (chap. ii.) that he "first discovered the gum elastic, which has been procured, as yet, only at Corisco, Gabun, and Kama." In 1854, Mr. Thompson (p. 112) found it in the Mendi country, near Sherbro; he describes it as a vine with dense bark, which yields the gum when hacked, and which becomes soft and porous when old. The juice is milk-white, thick, and glutinous, soon stiffening, darkening, and hardening without aid of art. I should like to see the raw material tried for making waterproofs in the tropics, where the best vulcanized articles never last. The Ndámbo tree has been traced a hundred miles inland from the Liberian Coast; that of the Gallinas and Sherbro is the best; at St. Paul's River it is not bad; but on the Junk River it is sticky and little prized. The difficulty everywhere is to make the negro collect it, and, when he does, to sell it unadulterated: in East Africa he uses the small branches of the ficus for flogging canes, but will not take the trouble even to hack the "Mpira" tree.

At a brook of the sweetest water, purling over the cleanest and brightest of golden sands, we filled the canteens, this being the last opportunity for some time. Forest walks are thirsty work during the hot season; the air is close, fetid, and damp with mire; the sea-breeze has no power to enter, and perspiration streams from every pore. After heavy rains it is still worse, the surface of the land is changed, and paths become lines of dark puddles; the nullahs, before dry, roll muddy, dark-brown streams, and their mouths streak the sea with froth and scum. Hardly a living object meets the eye, and only the loud, whirring flight of some large bird breaks the dreary silence. The music of the surf now sounded like the song of the sea-shell as we crossed another rough prism of stone and bush, whose counter-slope fell gently into a sand-flat overgrown with Ipomaa and other bright flowering plants. After walking about an hour (equal to 2·50 miles) between south and south-west, we saluted the pleasant aspect of θάλασσα with a general cheer. Northwards lay Point Ipizarala, southways Nyonye, both looking like tree-clumps rising from the waves. I could not sufficiently admire, and I shall never forget the exquisite loveliness of land and sea; the graceful curve of the beach, a hundred feet broad, fining imperceptibly away till lost in the convexity of waters. The morning sun, half way to the zenith, burned bright in a cloudless sky, whilst in the east and west distant banks of purple mist coloured the liquid plain with a cool green-blue, a celadon tint that reposed the eye and the brain. The porpoise raised in sport his dark, glistening back to the light of day, and plunged into the cool depths as if playing off the "amate sponde" of the Mediterranean; and sandpipers and curlews, the latter wild as ever, paced the smooth, pure floor. The shore-line was backed by a dark vegetable wall, here and there broken and fronted by single trees, white mangroves tightly corded down, and raised on stilted roots high above the tide. Between wood and wave lay powdered sandstone of lively yellow, mixed with bright white quartz and débris of pink shells. Upon the classic shores of Greece I should have thought of Poseidon and the Nereids; but the lovely scene was in unromantic Africa, which breeds no such visions of

"The fair humanities of old religion."

Resuming our road, we passed the ruins of an "Olako," the khámbí of East Africa, a temporary encampment, whose few poles were still standing under a shady tree. We then came upon a block-aded lagoon; the sea-water had been imprisoned by a high bank which the waves had washed up, and it will presently be released by storms from the south-west. Near the water, even at half-ebb, we find the floor firm and pleasant; it becomes loose walking at high tide, and the ribbed banks are fatiguing to ascend and descend under a hot sun and in reeking air. A seine would have supplied a man-of-war in a few hours; large turtle is often turned; in places young ones about the size of a dollar scuttled towards the sea, and Hotaloya brought a nest of eggs, which, however, were too high in flavour for the European palate. The host of crabs lining the water stood alert, watching our approach, and when we came within a hundred yards they hurried sideways into the safer sea—the scene reminded me of the days when, after "tiffin," we used to "már kankrás" on the Clifton Sands in the Unhappy Valley.

Presently we came to a remarkable feature of this coast, the first specimen of which was seen at Point Ovindo in the Gaboon River. The Iberian explorers called them "Sernas," fields or downs, opposed to Corôas, sand-dunes or hills. They are clearings in the jungle made by Nature's hand, fenced round everywhere, save on the sea side, by tall walls of dark vegetation; averaging perhaps a mile long by 200 yards broad, and broken by mounds and terraces regular as if worked by art. These prairies bear a green sward, seldom taller than three feet, and now ready for the fire,—here and there the verdure is dotted by a tree or two. It is universally asserted that they cannot be cultivated; and, if this be true, the cause would be worth investigating. In some places they are perfectly level, and almost flush with the sea; in others they swell gently to perhaps 100 feet; in other parts, again, they look like scarps and earthworks, remarkably resembling the lower parasitic craters of a huge volcano; and here and there they are pitted with sinks like the sea-board of Loango. These savannahs (savánas) add an indescribable charm to the Gaboon Coast, especially when the morning and evening suns strike them with slanting rays, and compel them to stand out distinct from the setting of eternal emerald. The aspect of the downs is civilized as the banks of the Solent; and the coast wants nothing to complete the "fine, quiet old-country picture in the wilds of Africa" but herds of kine grazing upon leas shining with a golden glory, or a country seat, backed by the noble virgin forest, such a *bosquet* as Europe never knew.

After another hour's walk, which carried us about three miles, we sighted in one of these *prairillons* a clump of seventeen huts. A negro in European clothes, after prospecting the party through a ship's glass, probably the gift of some slaver, came down to meet us, and led the way to his "town." Finding his guest an Englishman, the host, who spoke a few words of French and Portuguese, at once began to talk of his "summer *gîte,*" where *pirogues* were cut out, and boats were built; there were indeed some signs of this *industrie*, but all things wore the true Barracoon aspect. Two very fine girls were hid behind the huts, but did not escape my factotum's sharp eyes; and several of the doors were carefully padlocked: the pretty faces had been removed when he returned. This coast does an active retail business with São Thomé and the Ilha do Principe,—about Cape Lopez the "ebony trade" still, I hear, flourishes on a small scale.

During our halt for breakfast at the barracoon, we were visited by Petit Denis, a son of the old king. His village is marked upon the charts some four miles south-south-east of his father's; but at this season all the royalties, we are assured, affect the sea-shore. He was dressed in the usual loin-wrap, under a broadcloth coat, with the French official buttons. Leading me mysteriously aside, he showed certificates from the officials at Le Plateau, dating from 1859, recommending him strongly as a shipbroker for collecting *émigrants libres*, and significantly adding, *les nègres ne manquent pas*. Petit Denis's face was a study when I told him that, being an Englishman, a dozen negroes were not worth to me a single "Njína." Slave cargoes of some eight to ten head are easily canoed down the rivers, and embarked in schooners for the islands: the latter sadly want hands, and should be assisted in setting on foot a system of temporary immigration.

At 10.45 A.M. we resumed our march. The fiery sun had sublimated black clouds, the north-east quarter looked ugly, and I wished to be housed before the storm burst. The coast appeared populous; we met many bushmen, who were perfectly civil, and showed no fear, although some of them had probably never seen a white face. All were armed with muskets, and carried the usual hunting talismans, horns and iron or brass bells, hanging from the neck before and behind. We crossed four sweet-water brooks, which, draining the high banks, flowed fast and clear down cuts of loose, stratified sand, sometimes five feet deep: the mouths opened to the north-west, owing to the set of the current from the south-west, part of the great Atlantic circulation running from the Antarctic to the equator. Those which are not bridged with fallen trees must be swum during the rains, as the water is often waist-deep. Many streamlets, shown by their feathery fringes of bright green palm, run along the shore before finding an outlet; they are excellent bathing places, where the salt water can be washed off the skin. The sea is delightfully tepid, but it is not without risk,—it becomes deep within biscuit-toss, there is a strong under-tow, and occasionally an ugly triangular fin may be seen cruizing about in unpleasant proximity. As our naked feet began to blister, we suddenly turned to the left, away from the sea; and, after crossing about 100 yards of *prairillon*, one of the prettiest of its kind, we found ourselves at Bwá-mánge, the village of King Lángobúmo. It was then noon, and we had walked about three hours and a half in a general south-south-west direction.

His majesty's hut was at the entrance of the village, which numbered five scattered and unwalled sheds. He at once led us to his house, a large bamboo hall, with several inner sleeping rooms for the "Harím;" placed couch, chair, and table, the civilization of the slave-trade; brought wife No. 1 to shake hands, directed a fowl to be killed, and, sitting down, asked us the news in French. As a return for our information, he told us that the Gorilla was everywhere to be found, even in the bush behind his town. The rain coming down heavily, I was persuaded to pass the night there, the king offering to beat the bush with us, to engage hunters, and to find a canoe which would carry the party to Sánga-Tánga, landing us at all the likely places. I agreed the more willingly to the suggestion of a cruize, as my Mpongwe fashionables, like the Congoese, and unlike the Yorubans, proved to be bad and untrained walkers; they complained of sore feet, and they were always anticipating attacks of fever.

When the delicious sea-breeze had tempered the heat, we set out for the forest, and passed the afternoon in acquiring a certainty that we had again been "done." However, we saw the new guides, and supplied them with ammunition for the next day. The evening was still and close; the Ifúrú (sandflies) and the Nchúná (a red gad-fly) were troublesome as usual, and at night the mosquitoes phlebotomized us till we hailed the dawn.[1] A delightful bath of salt followed by fresh water, effectually quenched the fiery irritation of these immundicities.

Wednesday, as we might have expected, was wasted, although the cool and cloudy weather was perfection for a cruize. As we sat waiting for a boat, a youth rushed in breathless, reporting that he had just seen an "ole man gorilla" sitting in a tree hard by. I followed him incredulously at first, but presently the crashing of boughs and distant grunts, somewhat like huhh! huhh! huhh! caused immense excitement. After half a day's hard work, which resulted in nothing, I returned to Bwámánge, and met the "boat-king," whose

[1] I did not see the Iboko, which M. du Chaillu (chap. xvi.) calls the "boco;" but, from the native description, I determined it to be the tsetse. He names the sandfly (chap. xvi.) "igoo-gouai." His "ibolai" or "mangrove fly" is "owole" in the singular, and "iwole" in the plural. The wasp, which he terms "eloway," is known to the Mpongwe people as "ewogoni."

capital was an adjacent settlement of three huts. He was in rags, and my diary might have recorded, *Reçu un roi dans un très fichu état.* He was accompanied by a young wife, with a huge *toupet,* and a gang of slaves, who sat down and stared till their eyes blinked and watered. For the loan of his old canoe he asked the moderate sum of fifteen dollars per diem, which finally fell to two dollars; but there was a suspicious reservation anent oars, paddles and rudder, mast and sail.

Meanwhile the sanguine Selim compelled his guide to keep moving in the direction of the gorilla's grunt, and explaining his reluctance to advance by the fear of meeting the brute in the dark. Savage Africa, however, had as usual the better of the game, and showed his 'cuteness by planting my factotum in mud thigh-deep. After dark Forteune returned. He had fired at a huge njína, but this time the cap had snapped. As the monster was close, and had shown signs of wrath, we were expected to congratulate Nimrod on his escape. Kindly observe the neat gradations, the artistic sorites of Mpongwe lies.

At 7.30 A.M. on the next day the loads were placed upon the crew's heads, and we made for the village, where the boat was still drawn up. The "monoxyle" was full of green-brown rain water, the oar-pins were represented by bits of stick, and all the furniture was wanting. After a time, the owner, duly summoned, stalked down from his hut, and began remarking that there was still a "palaver" on the stocks. I replied by paying him his money, and ordering the craft to be baled and launched. It was a spectacle to see the bushmen lying upon their bellies, kicking their heels in the air, and yep-yep-yeping uproariously when Forteune, their master, begged of them to bear a hand. Dean Presto might have borrowed from them a hint for his Yahoos. The threat to empty the Alugu (rum) upon the sand was efficacious. One by one they rose to work, and in the slowest possible way were produced five oars, of which one was sprung, a ricketty rudder, a huge mast, and a sail composed half of matting and half of holes. At the last moment, the men found that they had no "chop;" a franc produced two bundles of sweet manioc, good travelling food, as it can be eaten raw, but about as nutritious as Norwegian bark. At the last, last moment, Lángobúmo, who was to accompany us, remembered that he had neither fine coat nor umbrella,—indispensable for dignity, and highly necessary for the delicacy of his complexion, which was that of an elderly buffalo. A lad was started to fetch these articles; and he set off at a hand-gallop, making me certain that behind the first corner he would subside into a saunter, and lie down to rest on reaching the huts.

Briefly, it was 9 A.M. before we doubled Point Nyonye, which had now been so long in sight. With wind, tide, and current dead against us, we hugged the shore where the water is deep. The surf was breaking in heavy sheets upon a reef or shoal outside, and giving ample occupation to a hovering flock of fish-eating birds. Whilst returning over water smooth as glass I observed the curious effect of the current. Suddenly a huge billow would rear like a horse, assume the shape of a giant cobra's head, fall forward in a mass of foam, and subside gently rippling into the calm surface beyond; the shadowy hollow of the breakers made them appear to impinge upon a black rock, but when they disappeared the sea was placid and unbroken as before. This is, in fact, the typical "roller" of the Gaboon coast—a happy hunting ground for slavers and a dangerous place for cruizers to attempt. As the sea-breeze came up strong, the swell would have swamped a European boat; but our conveyance, shaped like a ship's gig, but Dalmatian or Dutchman-like in the bows, topped the waves with the buoyancy of a cork, and answered her helm as the Arab obeys the bit. To compact grain she added small specific gravity, and, though stout and thick, she advanced at a speed of which I could hardly believe her capable.

Past Nyonye the coast forms another shallow

bay, with about ten miles of chord, in every way a copy of its northern neighbour—the same scene of placid beauty, the sea rimmed with opalline air, pink by contrast with the ultramarine blue; the limpid ether overhead; the golden sands, and the emerald verdure—a Circe, however, whose caress is the kiss of death. The curve is bounded south by Point Dyánye, which appeared to retreat as we advanced. At 2 P.M., when the marvellous clearness of the sky was troubled by a tornado forming in the north-east, we turned towards a little inlet, and, despite the heavy surf, we disembarked without a ducking. A creek supplied us with pure cold water, a spreading tree with a roof, and the soft clean shore with the most luxurious of couches—at 3 P.M. I could hardly persuade myself that an hour had flown.

As we approached Dyánye, at last, a village hoisted the usual big flag on the normal tall pole, and with loud cries ordered us to land. Lángo-búmo, who was at the helm, began obeying, when I relieved him of his charge. Seeing that our course was unaltered, a large and well-manned canoe put off, and the rest of the population walked down shore. I made signs for the stranger not to approach, when the head man, Angílah, asked me in English what he had done to offend me, and peremptorily insisted upon my sleeping at his village. All these places are looking forward to the blessed day when a trader, especially a white trader, shall come to dwell amongst the "sons of the soil," and shall fill their pockets with "trust" money. On every baylet and roadstead stands the *Casa Grande*, a large empty bungalow, a factory in embryo awaiting the Avatar; but, instead of attracting their "merchant" by collecting wax and honey, rubber and ivory, the people will not work till he appears. Consequently, here, as in Angola and in the lowlands of the Brazil, it is a slight to pass by without a visit; and jealousy, a ruling passion amongst Africans, suggests that the stranger is bound for another and rival village. They wish, at any rate, to hear the news, to gossip half the night, to drink the Utangáni's rum, and to claim a cloth for escorting him, will he, nill he, to the next settlement. But what could I do? To indulge native prejudice would have stretched my cruize to a fortnight; and I had neither time, supplies, nor stomach for the task. So Lángobúmo was directed to declare that they had a "wicked white man" on board who e'en would gang his ane gait, who had no goods but weapons, and who wanted only to shoot a njína, and to visit Sánga-Tánga, where his brother "Mpolo" had been. All this was said in a sneaking, deprecating tone, and the crew, though compelled to ply their oars, looked their regrets at the exceedingly rude and unseemly conduct of their Utangáni. Angílah followed chattering till he had learned all the novelties; at last he dropped aft, growling much, and promising to receive me at Sánga-Tánga next morning—not as a friend. On our return, however, he prospected us from afar with the greatest indifference; we were empty-handed. There has been change since the days when Lieutenant Boteler, passing along this shore, was addressed by the canoe-men, "I say, you mate, you no big rogue? ship no big rogue?"

At 5 P.M. we weathered Point Dyánye, garnished, like Nyonye, with a threatening line of breakers; the boat-passage along shore was about 400 yards wide. Darkness came on shortly after six o'clock, and the sultry weather began to look ominous, with a huge, angry, black nimbus discharging itself into the glassy livid sea northwards. I suggested landing, but Lángobúmo was positive that the storm had passed westwards, and he objected, with some reason, that in the outer gloom the boat might be dashed to pieces. As we had not even a stone for an anchor, the plea proved valid. We guided ourselves, by the fitful flashes of forked and sheet lightning combined, towards a ghostly point, whose deeper blackness silhouetted it against the shades. Suddenly the boat's head was turned inland; a huge breaker, foaming along our gunwales, drove us forwards like the downwards motion of a "swing-swong," and, before we knew where we were, an ugly little bar had been crossed on the top of the curling scud. We could see the forest on both sides, but there was not light enough to trace the river line; I told Hotaloya to tumble out; "Plenty shark here, mas'r," was the only answer. We lost nearly half an hour of most valuable time in pottering and groping before all had landed.

At that moment the rain-clouds burst, and in five minutes after the first spatter all were wet to the skin. Selim and I stood close together, trying to light a match, when a sheet of white fire seemed to be let down from the black sky, passing between us with a simultaneous thundering crash and rattle, and a sulphurous smell, as if a battery had been discharged. I saw my factotum struck down whilst in the act of staggering and falling myself; we lay still for a few moments, when a mutual inquiry showed that both were alive, only a little shaken and stunned; the sensation was simply the shock of an electrical machine and the discharge of a Woolwich infant —greatly exaggerated.

We then gave up the *partie;* it was useless to contend against Jupiter Tonans as well as Pluvialis. I opened my bedding, drank a "stiffener" of raw cognac, wrapped myself well, and at once fell asleep in the heavy rain, whilst the crew gathered under the sail. The gentlemen who stay at home at ease may think damp sheets dangerous, but Malvern had long ago taught me the perfect safety of the wettest bivouac, provided that the body remains warm. At Fernando Po, as at Zanzibar, a drunken sailor after a night in the gutter will catch fever, and will probably die. But he has exposed himself to the inevitable chill after midnight, he is unacclimatized, and both places are exceptionally deadly—to say nothing of the liquor. The experienced African traveller awaking with a chilly skin, swallows a tumbler of cold water, and rolls himself in a blanket till he perspires; there is only one alternative.

Next day I arose at 4 A.M., somewhat cramped and stiff, but with nothing that would not yield to half a handful of quinine, a cup of coffee well "laced," a pipe, and a roaring fire. Some country people presently came up, and rated us for sleeping in the bush; we retorted in kind, telling them that they should have been more wide-awake. Whilst the boat was being baled, I walked to the shore, and prospected our day's work. The forest showed a novel feature; flocks of cottony mist-clouds curling amongst the trees, like opals scattered upon a bed of emeralds; a purple haze banked up the western horizon, whilst milk-white foam drew a delicate line between the deep yellow sand and the still deeper blue. Far to the south lay the Serna or *prairillon* of Sánga-Tánga, a rolling patch, "or, on a field vert," backed by the usual dark belt of the same, and fronted by straggling dots that emerged from the wave—they proved to be a thin line of trees along shore. We were lying inside the mouth of the "Habanyá," *alias* the Shark River, which flows along the south of a high grassy dome, streaked here and there with rows of palms, and broken into the semblance of a verdure-clad crater. According to the people the Nkonje (*Squalus*) here is not a dangerous "sea-tiger" unless a man wear red or carry copper bracelets; it is caught with hooks and eaten as by the Chinese and the Suri Arabs. The streamlet is a favourite haunt of the hippopotamus; a small one dived when it sighted us, and did not reappear. It was the only specimen that I saw during my three years upon the West African Coast,—a great contrast to that of Zanzibar, where half a dozen may be shot in a single day. The musket has made all the difference.

At 6 A.M. on Friday, March 28, the boat was safely carried over the bar of Shark River, and we found ourselves once more hugging the shore southwards. The day was exceptional for West Africa, and much like damp weather at the end of an English May; the grey air at times indulged us with a slow drizzle. After two hours we passed another maritime village, where the farce of yesterday evening was re-acted, but this time with more vigour. Ignorant of my morning's private work, Hotaloya swore that it was Sánga-Tánga. I complimented him upon his proficiency in lying, and poor Lángobúmo, almost in tears, confessed that he had pointed out to me the real place. Whereupon Hotaloya began pathetically to reproach him for being thus prodigal of the truth. Núrya, the "head trader," coming down to the beach, with dignity and in force told me in English that I must land, and was chaffed accordingly. He then blustered and threatened instant death, at which it was easy to laugh. About 10 A.M. we lay off our destination, some ten miles south of Dyánye Point. It was a beautiful site, the end of a grassy dune, declining gradually toward the tree-fringed sea; the yellow slopes, cut by avenues and broken by dwarf table-lands, were long afterwards recalled to my memory, when sighting the fair but desolate scenery south of Paraguayan Asuncion. These downs appear to be a sea-coast raised by secular upheaval, and much older than the flat tracts which encroach upon the Atlantic. We could now understand the position of the town which figures so largely in the squadron-annals of the equatorial shore; it was set upon a hillock, whence the eye could catch the approaching sail of the slaver, and where the flag could be raised conspicuously in token of no cruiser being near.

But the glory had departed from Sánga-Tánga (Peel-White? Strip-White?); not a trace of the town remained, the barracoons had disappeared, and all was innocent as upon the day of its creation. A deep silence reigned where the song of joy and the shrieks of torture had so often been answered by the voice of the forest, and Eternal Nature had ceased to be disturbed by the follies and crimes of man.

Sánga-Tánga was burned down, after the fashion of these people, when Mbango, whom Europeans called "Pass-all," King of the Urungu, who extend up the right bank of the Ogobe, passed away from the sublunary world. King Pass-all had completed his education in Portugal: a negro never attains his highest potential point of villany without a tour through Europe; and thus he rose to be the greatest slave-dealer in this slave-dealing scrap of the coast. In early life he protected the Spanish pirates who fled to Cape Lopez, after plundering the American brig "Mexico:" they were at last forcibly captured by Captain (the late Admiral) Trotter, R.N.; passed over to the United States, and finally hanged at Boston, during the Presidency of General Jackson. Towards the end of his life he became paralytic, like King Pepple of Bonny, and dangerous to the whites as well as to the blacks under his rule. The people, however, still speak highly of him, generosity being a gift which everywhere covers a multitude of sins. He was succeeded by one of his sons, who is favourably mentioned, but who soon followed him to the grave. I saw another, a boy, apparently a slave to a Mpongwe on the coast, and the rest of the family is scattered far and wide. Since Pass-all's death the "peddlers in human flesh and blood" have gone farther south: men spoke of a great depot at the Mpembe village on the banks of the Nazareth River, where a certain Ndábúliya is aided and abetted by two Utangáni. Now that "'long-sea" exportation has been completely suppressed, their only markets must be the two opposite islands.

South of Sánga-Tánga, lay a thin line of deeper blue, Fetish Point, the eastern projection of Cape Lopez Bay. From Mbango's Town it is easy to see the western headland, Cape Lopez, whose low outliers of sand and trees gain slowly but surely upon the waters of the Atlantic. I deferred a visit until a more favourable time, and—that time never came.

Cape Lopez is said to have considerable advantages for developing trade, but the climate appears adverse. A large Catholic mission, described by Barbot, was established here by the Portuguese: as in the Congo, nothing physical of it remains.

But Mr. Wilson is rather hard when he asserts that *all* traces have disappeared—they survive in superior 'cuteness of the native.

Little need be said about our return, which was merrier than the outward bound trip. Wind, tide, and current were now in our favour, and we followed the chords, not the arcs, of the several bays. At 9.30 P.M. we gave a wide berth to the rollers off Point Nyonye and two hours afterwards we groped through the outer darkness into Bwámánge, where the good Azízeh and Asúnye, who came to receive us, shouted with joy. On the next day another "gorilla palaver," when a large male was reported to have been shot without a shadow of truth, detained me: it was the last straw which broke the patient camel's back. After "dashing" to old King Lángobúmo one cloth, one bottle of absinthe, two heads of tobacco, and a clay pipe, we set out betimes for the fifteen miles' walk to Mbátá. Various obstacles delayed us on the way, and the shades of evening began to close in rapidly; night already reigned over the forest. Progress under such circumstances requires the greatest care; as in the streets of Damascus, one must ever look fixedly at the ground, under penalty of a shaking stumble over cross-bars of roots, or fallen branches hidden by grass and mud. And the worst of these wet walks is that, sooner or later, they bring on swollen feet, which the least scratch causes to ulcerate, and which may lame the traveller for weeks. They are often caused by walking and sitting in wet shoes and stockings; it is so troublesome to pull off and pull on again after wading and fording, repeated during every few hundred yards, that most men tramp through the brooks and suffer in consequence. Constant care of the feet is necessary in African travel, and the ease with which they are hurt—sluggish circulation, poor food and insufficient stimulants being the causes—is one of its *déplaisirs.* The people wash and anoint these wounds with palm oil: a hot bath, with pepper-water, if there be no rum, gives more relief, and caustic must sometimes be used.

We reached Mbátá at 6.15 P.M., and all agreed that two hours of such forest-walking do more damage than five days along the sands.

Since my departure from the coast, French naval officers, travellers and traders, have not been idle. The Marquis de Compiègne, who returned to France in 1874, suffering from ulcerated legs, had travelled up the Fernão Vaz, and its tributary the highly irregular Ogobai, Ogowaï, or Ogowé (Ogobe); yet, curious to remark, all his discoveries are omitted by Herr Kiepert. His furthest point was 213 kilometres east of "San Quita" (Sankwita), a village sixty-one kilometres north (??) of Pointe Fétiche, near Cape Lopez; but wars and receding waters prevented his reaching the confluence where the Ivindo fork enters the north bank of the Ogobe. He made observations amongst the "Kamma" tribe, which differs from the Bakele and other neighbours. M. Guirold, commanding a cruiser, was also sent to the estuary of the Rembo or Fernão Vaz, into which the Mpungule (N'poulounay of M. du Chaillu ?), ascended only by M. Aymès, discharges. The explorers found many shoals and shifting sands before entering the estuary; in the evening they stopped at the Ogobe confluence, where a French seaman was employed in custom-house duties. M. de Compiègne, after attending many palavers, was duly upset when returning to the ship.

On the Fernão Vaz there are now (1873) five factories, each named after some French town: Paris Factory, however, had fallen to ruins, the traders having migrated 150 miles higher up the Kamma River. Here a certain drunken kinglet, "Rampano," breaks everything he finds in the house, and pays damages when he returns to his senses. On March 31st there was a violent quarrel between the women of two settlements, and the "reguli" embarked with all their host, to fight it out; Rampano was the victor, and after the usual palaver the vanquished was compelled to pay a heavy fine. M. du Chaillu's descriptions of the country, a park land dotted with tree-mottes, are confirmed; but the sport, excepting hippopotamus, was poor, and the negroes were found eating a white-faced monkey—mere cannibalism amongst the coast tribes. The fauna and flora of the Ogobe are those of the Gaboon, and the variety of beautiful parrots is especially remarked.

On January 9, 1874, M. de Compiègne passed from the Fernão Vaz through the Obango Canal into the Ogobe, which, bordered by Fetish rocks, flows through vast forests; his object was to study the manners and customs of the Kammas, a more important tribe than is generally supposed, far outnumbering the Urungus of the coast. Their country is large and contains many factories, the traders securing allies by marrying native women. The principal items of import are dry goods, guns, common spirits, and American tobacco; profits must be large, as what costs in France one franc eighty cents. here sells for ten francs' worth of goods. The exports are almost entirely comprised in gum mastic and ivory. At the factory of Mr. Watkins the traveller secured certain figures which he calls "idols"—they are by no means fitted for the drawing-room table. He also noticed the "peace of the household," a strip of manatus nerve, at times used by paterfamilias.

Mr. R. B. N. Walker, who made sundry excursions between 1866 and 1873, also wrote from Elobe that he had left the French explorers, MM. de Compiègne and Marche, on the Okanda River which M. du Chaillu believes to be the northern fork of the Ogobe. Their letters (Feb. 12, 1874) were dated from Osse in the Okanda country, where they had made arrangements with the kinglet for a journey to the "Otjebos," probably the Moshebo or Moshobo cannibals of the "Gorilla Book." The rocks, shoals, and stony bottom of the Ogobe reduced their rate of progress to three miles a day, and, after four wearisome stages, they reached a village of Bákele. Here they saw the slave-driving tribe "Okota," whose appearance did not prepossess them and whose chief attempted unsuccessfully to stop the expedition. They did not leave before collecting specimens of the language.

Further eastward, going towards the country of the Yalimbongo tribe, they found the Okanda River, which they make the southern fork, the Okono being the northern, descending from the mountains; here food was plentiful compared with Okota-land. The active volcano reported by Mr. R. B. N. Walker, 1873, was found to bear a lake upon the summit—which, in plutonic formations, would suggest an extinct crater. East of the Yalimbongo they came upon the Apingis, whom M. du Chaillu, after two visits, also placed upon the southern fork of the Ogobe. The tribe is described as small in stature, of mild habits, and fond of commerce; hence their plantations on the north or right bank of the river are plundered with impunity by the truculent "Oshieba" (Moshebo or Moshobo?). Further east the river, after being obstructed by rapids, broadens to a mile and becomes navigable—they were probably above the "Ghats." It is supposed to arise south in a lakelet called Tem or N'dua. A Bákele village was seen near Ochunga, a large riverine island; and thence they passed into the country of the mountaineer Okandas. They are described as fine men, but terrible sorcerers; their plantations of banana and maize are often plundered by the "Oshieba," the latter being now recognized as a kindred tribe of the Pahouin (Fá*n*).

CHAPTER VI.

VILLAGE LIFE IN PONGO-LAND.

THE next day was perforce a halt. Forteune and his wives did not appear till 9 A.M., when it was dead low water. I had lent Nimrod a double-barrelled gun during the march, and he was evidently anxious to found a claim upon the protracted usufruct. "Dashes" also had to be settled, and loads made up. The two women to whose unvarying kindness all my comfort had been owing, were made happy with satin-stripe, cassis, and the inevitable nicotiana. In an unguarded moment my soft heart was betrayed into giving a bottle of absinthe to the large old person who claimed to be Forteune's mamma. Expecting nothing, had nothing been offered she would not have complained; the present acted upon her violently and deleteriously; she was like the cabman who makes *mauvais sang* because he has asked and received only twice his fare; briefly, next morning she was too surly to bid us adieu.

When giving Forteune his "dash," I was curious to hear how he could explain the report about the dead gorilla shot the night before last: the truth of the old saying, "a black man is never fast for an excuse," was at once illustrated; the beast had been badly wounded, but it had dragged itself off to die. And where was the blood? The rain had washed the blood away!

Nimrod seemed chagrined at the poor end of so much trouble, but there was something in his look and voice suggesting a suppressed thought—these people, like the English and the Somal, show their innermost secrets in their faces. At last, I asked him if he was now willing to try the She-kyani country. He answered flatly, "No!" And why?

Some bushmen had bewitched him; he knew the fellow, and would quickly make "bob come up his side:" already two whites had visited him with a view of shooting gorillas; both had failed; it was "shame palaver!"

This might have been true, but it certainly was not the whole truth. I can hardly accept M. du Chaillu's explanation, that the Mpongwe, who attack the beasts with trade muskets and pebbles, will not venture into the anthropoid's haunts unless certain of their white employer's staunchness. What could that matter, when our Nimrod had an excellent weapon in his hand and a strong party to back him? Very likely Forteune was tired with walking, and five dollars per shot made the game not worth the candle. Again, perhaps the black diplomatist feared to overstock the market with Njínas, or to offend some regular customer for the sake of an "interloper." In these African lands they waste over a monkey's skin or a bottle of rum as much intrigue as is devoted to a contested election in England.

I then asked the guide if my staying longer would be of any use? He answered with a simple negative. Whilst the Utángáni remained the Mbunji (spell) would still work, but it would at once be broken by our departure, and he would prove it by sending down the first-fruits. This appeared to me to be mere Mpongwe "blague," but, curious to say, the sequel completely justified both assertions. He threw out a hint, however, about certain enemies and my "medicine," the arsenical soap; I need hardly say that it was refused.

When the palaver ended and the tide served, a fierce tornado broke upon us, and the sky looked grisly in the critical direction, north-east. Having no wish to recross the Gaboon River during a storm blowing a head wind, I resolved to delay my departure till the morrow, and amused myself with drawing from the nude a picture of the village and village-life in Pongo-land.

The Mpongwe settlements on the Gaboon River are neatly built, but without any attempt at fortification; for the most part each contains one family, or rather a chief and his dependants. In the larger plantation "towns," the abodes form a single street, ranging from 100 to 1,000 yards in length; sometimes, but rarely, there are cross streets; the direction is made to front the sea-breeze, and, if possible, to present a corner to storm-bearing Eurus. An invariable feature, like the arcaded loggie of old Venetian towns, is the Námpolo, or palaver-house, which may be described as the club-room of the village. An open *hangar*, like the Ikongolo or "cask-house" of the trading places, it is known by a fire always kept burning. The houses are cubes, or oblong squares, varying from 10 to 100 feet in length, according to the wealth and dignity of the owner; all are one-storied, and a few are raised on switch foundations. Most of them have a verandah facing the street, and a "compound" or cleared space in the rear for cooking and other domestic purposes. The walls are built by planting double and parallel rows of posts, the material being either bamboo or the mid-rib of a wine-giving palm (*Raphia vinifera*); to these uprights horizontal slats of cane are neatly lashed by means of the never-failing "tie-tie," bast-slips, runners, or llianas. For the more solid buildings thin "Mpávo," or bark slabs, are fitted in between the double posts; when coolness is required, their place is taken by mats woven with the pinnated leaves of sundry palms. This is a favourite industry with the women, who make two kinds, one coarse, the other a neat and close article, of rattan-tint until it becomes smoke-stained: the material is so cheap and comfortable, that many of the missionaries prefer it for walls to brick or boarding. The windows are mere holes in the mats to admit light, and the doors are cut with a Mpáno (adze) from a single tree trunk, which would be wilful waste if timber were ever wanting. The floor is sometimes sandy, but generally of hard and level tamped clay, to which the European would prefer boarding, and, as a rule, it is clean—no fear of pythogenie from here! The pent-shaped roof of rafters and thatch is water-tight except when the host of rats disturb it by their nocturnal gambols.

Rich men affect five or six rooms, of which the principal occupies the centre. The very poor must be contented with one; the majority have two. The "but" combines the functions of hall, dining-room, saloon and bachelor's sleeping quarters. The "ben" contains a broad bed for the married, a standing frame of split bamboo with mats for mattresses; it is usually mounted on props to defend it from the Nchu'u or white ants, and each has its mosquito bar, an oblong square, large enough to cover the whole couch and to reach the ground; the material is either fine grass-cloth, from the Ashíra country, a light stuff called "Mbongo," or calico and blue baft from which the stiffening has been washed out. It is far superior to the flimsy muslin affairs supplied in an Anglo-Indian outfit, or to the coarse matting used in Yoruba. Provided with this solid defence, which may be bought in any shop, one can indulge one's self by sleeping in the verandah without risk of ague or rheumatism. The "ben" always displays a pile of chests and boxes, which, though possibly empty, testify to the "respectability" of the household. In Hotaloya's I remarked a leather hat-case; he owned to me that he had already invested in a silk tile, the sign of chieftainship, but that being a "boy" he must grow older before he could wear it. The inner room can be closed with a strong door and a padlock; as even the window-hole is not admitted, the burglar would at once be detected. Except where goods are concerned, the Mpongwe have little respect for privacy; the women, in the presence of their husbands, never failed to preside at my simple toilette, and the girls of the villages would sit upon the bedside where lay an Utangání in almost the last stage of *déshabillé*.

The furniture of course varies; a rich man near the river will have tables and chairs, sofas, looking-glasses, and as many clocks, especially "Sam Slicks," as love or money can procure. Even the poorest affect a standing bedstead in the "ben," plank benches acting as couches in the "but," a sufficiency of mats, and pots for water and cooking. A free man never condescends to sit upon the ground; the low stool, cut out of a single block, and fancifully carved, is exactly that of the old Egyptians preserved by the modern East Africans; it dates from ages immemorial. The look of comparative civilization about these domiciles, doubtless the effect of the Portuguese and the slave trade, distinguishes them from the barbarous circular huts of the Kru-men, the rude clay walls of the Gold Coast, and the tattered, comfortless sheds of the Fernandian "Bube." They have not, however, that bandbox-like neatness which surprises the African traveller on the Camerones River.

The only domestic animals about these villages are dogs, poultry, and pigeons (fine blue rocks): I never saw in Pongo-land the goats mentioned by M. du Chaillu. The bush, however, supplies an abundance of "beef," and, as most South Africans, they have a word, Isángú (amongst the Mpongwes), or Ingwámbá (of the Cape Lopez people), to express that inordinate longing and yearning for the stimulus of meat diet, caused by the damp and depressing equatorial climate, of which Dr. Livingstone so pathetically complains. The settlements are sometimes provided with little plots of vegetables; usually, however, the plantations are distant, to preserve them from the depredations of bipeds and quadrupeds. They are guarded by bushmen, who live on the spot and, shortly before the rains all the owners flock to their farms, where, for a fortnight or so, they and their women do something like work. New grounds are preferred, because it is easier to clear them than to remove the tangled after-growth of ferns and guinea grass; moreover, they yield, of course, better crops. The plough has not yet reached Pongo-land; the only tools are the erem (little axe for felling), the matchet (a rude cutlass for clearing), the hoe, and a succedaneum for the dibble. After the bush has been burned as manure, and the seed has been sown, no one will take the trouble of weeding, and half the surface is wild growth.

Maize (*Zea mays*) has become common, and the people enjoy "bútás," or roasted ears. Barbot says that the soil is unfit for corn and Indian wheat; it is so for the former, certainly not for the latter. Rice has extended little beyond the model farms on the north bank of the river; as everywhere upon the West African Coast, it is coarser, more nutritious, and fuller flavoured than the

Indian. The cereals, however, are supplanted by plantains and manioc (cassava). The plantains are cooked in various ways, roast and boiled, mashed and broiled, in paste and in balls; when unripe they are held medicinal against dysentery. The manioc is of the white variety (*Jatropha Aypim seu utilissima*), and, as at Lagos, the root may be called the country bread: I never saw the poisonous or black manioc (*Jatropha manihot*), either in East or in West Africa, and I heard of it only once in Unyamwezi, Central Africa. Yet it is mentioned by all old travellers, and the sweet harmless variety gives very poor "farinha," *Anglicè* "wood meal."

The vegetables are "Mbongwe" (yams), koko or *Colocasia esculenta*, Occras (*Hibiscus esculentus*), squashes (pumpkins), cucumbers, beans of several sorts, and the sweet potato, an esculent disliked by Englishmen, but far more nutritious than the miserable "Irish" tuber. The ground-nut or pea-nut (*Arachis hypogæa*), the "pindar" of the United States, a word derived from Loango, is eaten roasted, and, as a rule, the people have not learned to express its oil. Proyart (Pinkerton, xvi. 551) gives, probably by misprint, "Pinda, which we call Pistachio." "Bird-peppers," as the small red species is called, grow wild in every bush; they are wholesome, and the people use them extensively. Tomatoes flourish almost spontaneously, and there is a bulbless native onion whose tops make excellent seasoning. Sugar-cane will thrive in the swamps, coffee on the hill-slopes: I heard of, but never saw ginger.

The common fruits are limes and oranges, mangoes, papaws, and pineapples, the gift of the New World, now run wild, and appreciated chiefly by apes. The forest, however, supplies a multitude of wild growths, which seem to distinguish this section of the coast, and which are eaten with relish by the people. Amongst them are the Sángo and Nefu, with pleasant acid berries; the Ntábá, described as a red grape, which will presently make wine; the olive-like Azyigo (Ozigo?); the filbert-like Kula, the "koola-nut" of M. du Chaillu ("Second Expedition," chap. viii.), a hard-shelled nux, not to be confounded with the soft-shelled kola (*Sterculia*); and the Aba, or wild mango (*Mango Gabonensis*), a pale yellow pome, small, and tasting painfully of turpentine. It is chiefly prized for its kernels. In February and March all repair to the bush for their mango-*vendange*, eat the fruit, and collect the stones: the insides, after being sun-dried, are roasted like coffee in a neptune, or in an earthern pot. When burnt chocolate colour, they are pounded to the consistency of thick honey, poured into a mould, a basket lined with banana leaves, and set for three days to dry in the sun: after this the cake, which in appearance resembles guava cheese, will keep through the year.

For use the loaf is scraped, and a sufficiency is added to the half-boiled or stewed flesh, the two being then cooked together: it is equally prized in meat broths, or with fish, dry and fresh; and it is the favoured kitchen for rice and the insipid banana. "Odika," the "Ndika" of the Bákele tribes, is universally used, like our "Worcester," and it may be called the one sauce of Gorilla-land, the local equivalent for curry, pepper-pot, or palm-oil chop; it can be eaten thick or thin, according to taste, but it must always be as hot as possible. The mould sells for half a dollar at the factories, and many are exported to adulterate chocolate and cocoa, which it resembles in smell and oily flavour. I regret to say that travellers have treated this national relish disrespectfully, as continentals do our "plomb-boudin:" Mr. W. Winwood Reade has chaffed it, and another Briton has compared it with "greaves."

At "Cockerapeak," or, to speak less unpoetically, when Alectryon sings his hymn to the dawn, the working bees of the little hive must be up and stirring, whilst the master and mistress enjoy the beauty-sleep. "Early to bed, and early to rise," is held only fit to make a man surly, and give him red eyes, by all wild peoples, who have little work, and who justly hold labour an evil less only than death. Amongst the Bedawin it is a sign of Shaykh-dom not to retire before dawn, and I have often heard the Somal "palavering" after midnight. As a rule the barbarian enjoys his night chat and smoke round the fire all the more because he drinks or dozes through the better part of the day. There is a physical reason for the preference. The absence of light stimulus, and the changes which follow sunset seem to develope in him a kind of night-fever as in the nervous temperament of Europe. Hence so many students choose the lamp in preference to the sun, and children mostly clamour when told at 8 o'clock to go to bed.

Shortly after sunrise the young ones are bathed in the verandah. Here also the mistress smooths her locks, rumpled by the night, "tittivates" her macaw-crest with the bodkin, and anoints her hair and skin with a *tantinet* of grease and palm oil. Some, but by no means all, proceed for ablution to the stream-side, and the girls fetch water in heavy earthen jars, containing perhaps two gallons; they are strung, after the Kru fashion, behind the back by a band passing across the forehead. When we meet them they gently say "Mbolo!" (good morning), or "Oresa" (are you well)? At this hour, however, all are not so civil, the seniors are often uncommonly cross and surly, and the *mollia tempora fandi* may not set in till after the first meal—I have seen something of the kind in England. The sex, unpolitely said to have one fibre more in the heart and one cell less in the brain, often engages in a violent wordy war; the tornado of wrath will presently pass over, and leave clear weather for the day. In the evening, when the electric fluid again gathers heavily, there will be another storm. Meanwhile, superintended by the mistress, all are occupied with the important duty of preparing the morning meal. It is surprising how skilful are these heaven-born cooks; the excellent dishes they make out of "half-nothing." I preferred the *cuisine* of Forteune's wives to that of the Plateau, and, after finding that money was current in the village, I never failed to secure their good offices.

The Mpongwe breakfast is eaten by the women in their respective verandahs, with their children and friends; the men also gather together, and prefer the open air. This feed would not only astonish those who talk about a "free breakfast-table," with its silly slops and bread-stuffs; it would satisfy a sharp-set Highlander. In addition to yams and sweet potatoes, plantains, and perhaps rice, there will be cooked mangrove-oysters fresh from the tree, a fry, or an excellent *bouillabaisse* of fish; succulent palaver sauce, or palm-oil chop; poultry and meat. The domestic fowl is a favourite; but, curious to say, neither here nor in any part of tropical Africa known to me have the people tamed the only gallinaceous bird which the Black Continent has contributed to civilization. The Guinea fowl, like the African elephant, remains wild. We know it to be an old importation in Europe, although there are traditions about its appearing in the fourteenth century, when Moslems sold it to Christians as the "Jerusalem cock," and Christians to Moslems as the "bird of Meccah." It must be the Greek meleagris, so called, says Ælian, from the sisters who wept a brother untimely slain; hence the tears upon its plume, suggesting the German Perl-huhn, and its frequent cries, which the Brazilians, who are great in the language of birds, translate *Sto fraca, sto fraca, sto fraca* (I'm weak). The Hausa Moslems make the Guinea fowl cry, "Kilkal! kilkal!" (Grammar by the Rev. F. J. Schön, London, Salisbury Square, 1862). It is curious to compare the difference of ear with which nations hear the cries of animals, and form their onomatopoetic, or "bow-wow" imitations. For instance, the North Americans express by "whip-poor-will" what the Brazilians call "João-corta-páo." The Guinea fowl may have been the "Afraa avis;" but that was a dear luxury amongst the Romans, though the Greek meleagris was cheap. The last crotchet about it is that of an African traveller, who holds it to be the peacock of Solomon's navies, completely ignoring the absolute certainty which the South-Indian word "Tukkiim" carries with it.

The Mpongwe will not eat ape, on account of its likeness to themselves. But they greatly enjoy game; the porcupine, the ground-hog (an Echymys), the white flesh of the bush pig (*Cricetomys*), and the beef of the Nyáre (*Bos brachyceros*); this is the "buffalo" or "bush-cow" of the regions south of Sierra Leone, and the empacassa of the Congo-Portuguese, whose "empacasseirs" or native archers, rural police and auxiliaries "of the second line," have as "guerra preta" (black militia) won many a victory. Their numbers in Angola have amounted to 30,000, and they aided in conquest like the Indian Sipahi (sepoy) and the Tupi of the older Brazil. Now they wear the Tánga or Pagne, a waist cloth falling to the knee, and they are armed with trade muskets and cartridge-boxes fastened to broad belts. Barbot calls the Nyáre a buffalo, and tells us that it was commonly shot at Sandy Point, where in his day elephants also abounded. Captain Boteler (ii. 379) well describes a specimen, which was killed by Dr. Guland, R.N., as exactly resembling the common cow of England, excepting that its proportions are far more "elegant."

This hearty breakfast is washed down with long drinks of palm wine, and followed by sundry pipes of tobacco; after which, happy souls! all enjoy a siesta, long and deep as that of Andine Mendoza; and they "kill time" as well as they can till evening. The men assemble in the club round the Námpolo-fire, where they chat and smoke, drink and doze; those who are Agriophagi or Xylobian Æthiopians, briefly called hunters, spend their days much like the race which Byron declared

> "Merely born
> To hunt and vote, and raise the price of corn."

The Pongo venator is up with the sun, and, if not on horseback, at least he is on the traces of game; sometimes he returns home during the hours of heat, when he knows that the beasts seek the shady shelter of the deepest forests; and, after again enjoying the "pleasures of the chase," he disposes of a heavy dinner and ends the day, sleep weighing down his eyelids and his brains singing with liquor. What he did yesterday that he does to-day, and what he does to-day that he shall do to-morrow; his intellectual life is varied only by a visit to town, where he sells his choice skins, drinks a great deal too much rum, and makes the purchases, ammunition and so forth, which are necessary for the full enjoyment of home and country life. At times also he joins a party of friends and seeks some happier hunting ground farther from his *campagne.*

Meanwhile the women dawdle through the day,

superintending their domestic work, look after their children's and their own toilette, tend the fire, attend to the cooking, and smoke consumedly. The idle sit with the men at the doors of their huts; those industriously disposed weave mats, and, whether lazy or not, they never allow their tongues and lungs a moment's rest. The slaves, male and female, draw water, cut fuel, or go to the distant plantations for yams and bananas; whilst the youngsters romp, play and tease the village idiot—there is one in almost every settlement. Briefly, the day is spent in idleness, except, as has been said, for a short time preceding the rains.

When the sun nears the western horizon, the hunter and the slaves return home, and the housewife, who has been enjoying the "coolth" squatting on her dwarf stool at her hut-door, and puffing the preparatory pipe, girds her loins for the evening meal, and makes every one "look alive." When the last rays are shedding their rich red glow over the tall black trees which hem in the village, all torpidity disappears from it. The fires are trimmed, and the singing and harping, which were languid during the hot hours, begin with renewed vigour. The following is a specimen of a boating-song:

(*Solo.*) "Come, my sweetheart!"
(*Chorus.*) "Haste, haste!"

(*Solo.*) "How many things gives the white man?"
(*Chorus chaunts all that it wants.*)

(*Solo.*) "What must be done for the white man?"
(*Chorus improvises all his requirements.*)

(*Solo.*) "How many dangers for the black girl?"
(*Chorus.*) "Dangers from the black and the white man!"

THE VILLAGE IDIOT.

The evening meal is eaten at 6 P.M. with the setting of the sun, whose regular hours contrast pleasantly with his vagaries in the northern temperates. And Hesperus brings wine as he did of old. Drinking sets in seriously after dark, and is known by the violent merriment of the men, and the no less violent quarrelling and "flyting" of the sex which delights in the "harmony of tongues." All then retire to their huts, and with chat and song, and peals of uproarious laughter and abundant horseplay, such as throwing minor articles at one another's heads, smoke and drink till 11 P.M. The scene is "Dovercourt, all speakers and no hearers." The night is still as the grave, and the mewing of a cat, if there were one, would sound like a tiger's scream.

The mornings and evenings in these plantation-villages would be delightful were it not for what the Brazilians call *immundicies.* Sandflies always swarm in places where underwood and tall grasses exclude the draughts, and the only remedy is clearing the land. Thus at St. Isabel or Clarence, Fernando Po, where the land-wind or the sea-breeze ever blows, the vicious little wretches are hardly known; on the forested background of mountain they are troublesome as at Nigerian Nufe. The bite burns severely, and presently the skin rises in bosses, lasting for days with a severe itching, which, if unduly resented, may end in inflammatory ulcerations—I can easily understand a man being laid up by their attacks. The animalcules act differently upon different constitutions. While mosquitoes hardly take effect, sand flies have often blinded me for hours by biting the circumorbital parts. The numbers and minuteness of this insect make it formidable. The people flap their naked shoulders with cloths or bushy twigs; Nigerian travellers have tried palm oil but with scant success, and spirits of wine applied to the skin somewhat alleviate the itching but has no prophylactic effect. Sandflies do not venture into the dark huts, and a "smudge" keeps them aloof, but the disease is more tolerable than the remedy of inflaming the eyes with acrid smoke and of sitting in a close box, by courtesy termed a room, when the fine pure air makes one pine to be beyond walls. After long endurance in hopes of becoming inoculated with the virus, I was compelled to defend myself with thick gloves, stockings and a muslin veil made fast to the hat and tucked in under the shirt. After sunset the sandflies retire, and the mosquito sounds her hideous trump; as has been said, however, Pongo-land knows how to receive her.

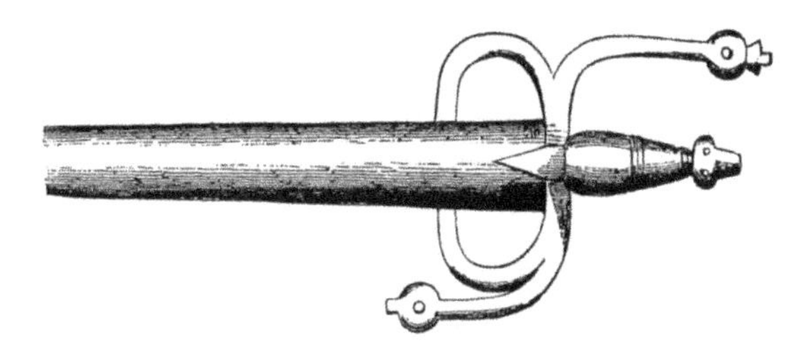

SWORD FROM THE INTERIOR.

CHAPTER VII.

RETURN TO THE RIVER.

ARLY on the last morning in March we roused the Kru-men; they were eager as ourselves to leave the "bush," and there was no delay in loading and launching the mission-boat. Forteune, Azízeh, and Asúnye were there to bid me God-speed, and Hotaloya did not fail to supply a fine example of Mpongwe irresolution.

That "sweet youth" had begged hard during the last week that I would take him to Fernando Po; carpenters were wanted for her Majesty's consulate, and he seemed to jump at the monthly pay of seven dollars—a large sum in these regions. On the night before departure he had asked me for half a sovereign to leave with his wives, and he made me agree to an arrangement that they should receive two dollars per mensem. In the morning I had alluded to the natural sorrow which his better semi-halves must feel, although the absence of groaning and weeping was very suspicious, and I had asked in a friendly way, "Them woman he make bob too much?"

"Ye', sar," he replied with a full heart, "he cry *too* much."

When the last batch had disappeared with the last box I walked up to him, and said, "Now, Andrews, you take hat, we go Gaboon."

Hotaloya at once assumed the maudlin expression and insipid *ricanement* of the Hindú charged with "Sharm kí bát" (something shameful).

"Please, mas'r, I no can go—Nanny Po he be too far—I no look my fader (the villain had three), them boy he say I no look 'um again!"

The wives had won the day, and words would have been vain. He promised hard to get leave from his papa and "grand-pap," and to join me after a last farewell at the Plateau. His face gave the lie direct to his speech, and his little manœuvre for keeping the earnest-money failed ignobly.

The swift brown stream carried us at full speed. "Captain Merrick" pointed out sundry short cuts, but my brain now refused to admit as truth a word coming from a Mpongwe. We passed some *bateaux pêcheurs*, saw sundry shoals of fish furrowing the water, and after two hours we were bumping on the rocks outlying Mombe Creek and Nenga Oga village. The passage of the estuary was now a pleasure, and though we grounded upon the shallows of "Voileliay Bay," the Kru-men soon lifted the heavy boat; the wind was fair, the tide was ebbing, and the strong current was in our favour. We reached Glass Town before midday, and after five hours, covering some twenty-two direct geographical miles, I found myself with pleasure under the grateful shade of the Factory. It need hardly be described, as it is the usual "bungalow" of the West African shore.

Twelve days had been expended upon 120 miles, but I did not regret the loss. A beautiful bit of country had been added to my mental Pinacothek, and I had satisfied my mind to a certain extent upon that *quæstio*, then *vexata*, the "Gorilla Book." Even before my trip the ethnological part appeared to me trustworthy, and, if not original, at any rate borrowed from the best sources. My journey assured me, from the specimen narrowly scrutinized, that both country and people are on the whole correctly described. The dates, however, are all in confusion: in the preface to the second edition, "October, 1859," became "October, 1858," and we are told that the excursions were transposed for the simple purpose of taking the reader from north to south. As in the case of most African travels, when instruments are not used, the distances must be reduced: in chapter xii. the Shekyani villages are placed sixty miles due east of Sánga-Tánga; whereas the map shows twenty. Mr. W. Winwood Reade declares that the Apingi country, the *ultima Thule* of the explorer, is distant from Ngumbi "four foot-days' journey;" as MM. de Compiègne and Marche have shown, the tribe in question extends far and wide. Others have asserted that seventy-five miles formed the maximum distance. But many of M. du Chaillu's disputed distances have been proved tolerably correct by MM. Serval and Griffon du Bellay, who were sent by the French government in 1862 to survey the Ogobe. A second French expedition followed shortly afterwards, under the charge of MM. Labigot and Touchard; and finally that of 1873, like all preceding it, failed to find any serious deviation from fact.

The German exploring expedition (July 25, 1873) confirms the existence of M. du Chaillu's dwarfs, the Obongo tribe, scoffed at in England because they dwell close to a fierce people of Patagonian proportions. The Germans report that they are called "Babongo," "Vambuta," and more commonly "Bari," or "Bali;" they dwell fourteen days' march from the mouth of the Luena, or River of Chinxoxo. I have not seen it remarked that these pygmies are mentioned by Andrew Battel Plinian at the end of the sixteenth century. "To the north-east of Mani Kesoch," he tells us, "are a kind of little people called Matimbas, who are no bigger than boys twelve years old, but are very thick, and live only upon flesh, which they kill in the woods with bows and darts." Of the Aykas south of the Welle River, discovered by Dr. Schweinfurth, I need hardly speak. It is not a little curious to find these confirmations of Herodotean reports about dwarfish tribes in the far interior, the Dokos and the Wabilikimo, so long current at Zanzibar Island, and so long looked upon as mere fables.

Our departure from Mbátá *had* broken the spell, and Forteune *did* keep his word; I was compelled in simple justice to cry "Peccavi." On the very evening of our arrival at Glass Town the youth Kángá brought me a noble specimen of what he called a Nchígo Mpolo, sent by Forteune's bushmen; an old male with brown eyes and dark pupils. When placed in an arm-chair, he ludicrously suggested a pot-bellied and patriarchal negro considerably the worse for liquor. From crown to sole he measured 4 feet 10¾ inches, and from finger-tip to finger-tip 6 feet 1 inch. The girth of the head round ears and eyebrows was 1 foot 11 inches; of the chest, 3 feet 2 inches; above the hip joints, 2 feet 4 inches; of the arms below the shoulder, 2 feet 5 inches; and of the legs, 2 feet 5 inches. Evidently these are very handsome proportions, considering what he was, and there was a suggestion of ear lobe which gave his countenance a peculiarly human look. He had not undergone the inhuman Hebrew-Abyssinian operation to which M. du Chaillu's gorillas had been exposed, and the proportions rendered him exceedingly remarkable.

That interesting anthropoid's career after death was one series of misfortunes, ending with being stuffed for the British Museum. My factotum sat up half the night skinning, but it was his first *coup d'essai.* In a climate like the Gaboon, especially during the rains, we should have turned the pelt "hairy side in," filled it with cotton to prevent shrinking, and, after painting on arsenic, have exposed it to the sun: better still, we should have placed it on a scaffolding, like a defunct Congoman, over a slow and smoky fire, and thus the fatty matter which abounds in the integuments would have been removed. The phalanges of the hands and feet, after being clean-scraped, were restored to their places, and wrapped with thin layers of arsenicated cotton, as is done to small animals, yet on the seventh day decomposition set in; it was found necessary to unsew the skin, and again to turn it inside out. The bones ought to have been removed, and not replaced till the coat was thoroughly dry. The skinned spoils were placed upon an ant-hill; a practice which recalls to mind the skeleton deer prepared by the emmets of the Hartz Forest, which taught Oken that the skull is(?) expanded vertebræ. We did not know that half-starved dogs and "drivers" will not respect even arsenical soap. The consequence of exposing the skeleton upon an ant-hill, where it ought to have been neatly cleaned during a night, was that the "Pariah" curs carried off sundry ribs, and the "parva magni formica laboris" took the trouble to devour the skin of a foot. Worse still: the skull, the brain, and the delicate members had been headed up in a breaker of trade rum, which was not changed till the seventh day. It was directed to an eminent member of the old Anthropological Society, and the most interesting parts arrived, I believe, soft, pulpy, and utterly useless. The subject seems to have been too sore for mentioning—at least, I never heard of it again.

The late Dr. John Edward Gray, of the British Museum, called this Nchígo Mpolo, from its bear-like masses of breast-pile, the "hairy Chimpanzee" (*Troglodytes vellerosus*). After my return home I paid it a visit, and could only think that the hirsute one was considerably "mutatus ab illo." The colour had changed, and the broad-chested, square-framed, pot-bellied, and portly old bully-boy of the woods had become a wretched pigeon-breasted, lean-flanked, shrunk-limbed, hungry-looking beggar. It is a lesson to fill out the skin, even with bran or straw, if there be nothing better—anything, in fact, is preferable to allowing the shrinkage which ends in this wretched caricature.

During my stay at Glass Town I was fortunate enough to make the acquaintance of the Rev. Messrs. Walker and Preston, of the Baraka Mission. The head-quarter station of the American Board of Foreign (Presbyterian) Missions was established on the Gaboon River in 1842 by the Rev. J. Leighton Wilson, afterwards one of the secretaries to the Society in New York. He had left the best of memories in "the River," and there were tales of his having manumitted in the Southern United States a small fortune of slaves without a shade of compulsion. His volume on West Africa, to which allusion has so often been made, contains a good bird's-eye of the inter-tropical coast, and might, with order, arrangement, and correction of a host of minor inaccuracies, become a standard work.

I have already expressed my opinion, founded upon a sufficiently long experience, that the United States missionary is by far the best man for the Western Coast, and, indeed, for dangerous tropical countries generally. Physically he is spare and hard, the nervous temperament being more strongly developed in him than in the bulbous and more bilious or sanguine European. He is better born, and blood never fails to tell. Again, he generally adopts the profession from taste, not because *il faut vivre.* He is better bred; he knows the negro from his childhood, and his education is more practical, more generally useful than that of his rivals. Moreover, I never yet heard him exclaim, "Capting, them heggs is 'igh!" Lastly he is more temperate and moderate in his diet: hitherto it has not been my fate to assist in carrying him to bed.

Perhaps the American missionary carries sobriety too far. In dangerous tropical regions, where there is little appetite and less nutritious diet, where exertion of mind and body easily exhaust vitality, and where "diffusible stimulants" must often take the place of solids, he dies first who drinks water. The second is the man who begins with an "eye-opener" of "brandy-pawnee," and who keeps up excitement by the same means through the day. The third is the hygienic sciolist, who drinks on principle poor "Gladstone" and thin French wines, cheap and nasty; and the survivor is the man who enjoys a *quantum suff.* of humming Scotch and Burton ales, sherry, Madeira, and port, with a modicum of cognac. This has been my plan in the tropics from the beginning, when it was suggested to me by the simplest exercise of the reasoning faculties. "A dozen of good port will soon set you up!" said the surgeon to me after fever. Then why not drink port before the fever?

I have said something upon this subject in "Zanzibar City, Island, and Coast" (i. p. 180), it will bear repetition. Joseph Dupuis justly remarks: "I am satisfied, from my own experience, that many fall victims from the adoption of a course of training improperly termed prudential; viz. a *sudden* change of diet from *ship's fare* to a scanty sustenance of vegetable matter (rejecting even a moderate proportion of wine), and seclusion in their apartments from the sun and atmosphere."

An immense mass of nonsense, copied in one "authority" from another, was thrown before the public by books upon diet, until the "Physiology of Common Life" (George Henry Lewes) discussed Liebig's brilliant error in considering food chemically, and not physiologically. The rest assume his classification without reserve, and work from the axiom that heat-making, carbonaceous and non-nitrogenous foods (*e.g.* fat and sugars), necessary to support life in the arctic and polar regions, must be exchanged for the tissue-making, plastic or nitrogenous (vegetables), as we approach the equator. They are right as far as the southern temperates, their sole field of observation; they greatly err in all except the hot, dry parts of the tropics. Why, a Hindoo will drink at a sitting a tumbler of glí (clarified butter), and the European who would train for wrestling after the fashion of Hindostan, as I attempted in my youth, on "native" sweetmeats and sugared milk, will be blind with "melancholia" in a week. The diet of the negro is the greasiest possible, witness his "palm-oil chop" and "palaver sauce;" his craving for meat, especially fat meat, is a feeling unknown to Europe. And how simple the reason. Damp heat demands almost as much carbon as damp or dry cold.

Return we to the Baraka Mission. The name is a corruption of "barracoon;" in the palmy days of the trade slave-pens occupied the ground now covered by the chapel, the schoolroom, and the dwelling-house, and extended over the site of the factory to the river-bank. The place is well chosen. Immediately beyond the shore the land swells up to a little rounded hill, clean and grassy like that about Sánga-Tánga. The soil appears poor, and yet around the mission-house there are some fine wild figs, one a huge tree, although not a score of years old; the bamboo clump is magnificent, and the cocoas, oranges, and mangoes are surrounded by thick, fragrant, and luxuriant quickset hedges of well-trimmed lime.

A few words concerning the banana of this coast, which we find so flourishing at Baraka. An immense god-send to the Gaboon, it is well known to be the most productive of all food, 100 square yards of it giving annually nearly 2,000 kilogrammes of food far more nutritious than the potato. Here it is the *musa sapientum*, the banana de Soã Thomé, which has crossed over to the Brazil, and which is there known by its sharper leaves and fruit, softer and shorter than the indigenous growth. The plant everywhere is most vigorous in constant moist heat, the atmosphere of a conservatory, and the ground must be low and wet, but not swampy. The best way of planting the sprouts is so to dispose them that four may form the corners of a square measuring twelve feet each side; the common style is some five feet apart. The raceme, which appears about the sixth to the tenth month, will take sixty days more to ripen; good stocks produce three and more bunches a year, each weighing from twenty to eighty pounds. The stem, after fruiting, should be cut down, in order to let the others enjoy light and air, and the oftener the plants are removed to fresh ground the better.

The banana, when unripe, is white and insipid; it is then baked under ashes till it takes a golden colour, and, like a cereal, it can be eaten as bread. A little later it is boiled, and becomes a fair vegetable, tasting somewhat like chestnuts, and certainly better than carrots or turnips. Lastly, when softer than a pear, it is a fruit eaten with milk or made into *beignets*. I have described the plantain-cider in "Lake Regions of Central Africa" (ii. 287). The fruit contains sugar, gum, and acids (malic and gallic); the rind, which is easily detached when ripe, stains cloth with ruddy grey rusty colour, by its tannin, gallic, and acetic acids.

The Baraka Mission has had several out-stations. One was at a ruined village of Fá*n*, which we shall presently pass on the right bank of the river. The second was at Ikoi, a hamlet distant about fifteen (not twenty-five) miles, upon a creek of the same name, which enters the Gaboon behind Point Ovindo, and almost opposite Konig Island. A third is at Anenge-nenge, *vulgò* Inenge-nenge,—"nenge" in Mpongwe, and anenge in Bákele, meaning island,—situated forty (not 100) miles up the main stream; here a native teacher still resides. The Baraka school now (1862) numbers thirty scholars, and there are twelve to fifteen communicants. The missionaries are our white "labourers;" but two of them, the Revs. Jacob Best and A. Bushnell, are absent in the United States for the benefit of their health.

My first visit to the Rev. William Walker made me regret my precipitate trip to Mbátá: he told me what I now knew, that it was the wrong line, and that I should have run two or three days up the Rembwe, the first large influent on the southern bank of the Gaboon. He had come out to the River in 1842, and had spent twenty years of his life in Africa, with occasional furloughs home. He greatly interested me by a work which he was preparing. The Gaboon Mission had begun its studies of the many native dialects by the usual preparatory process of writing grammars and vocabularies; after this they had published sundry fragmentary translations of the Scriptures, and now they aimed at something higher. After spending years in building and decorating the porticoes of language, they were ambitious of raising the edifice to which it is only an approach; in other words, of explaining the scholarship of the tongue, the spirit of the speech.

"Language," says the lamented Dr. O. E. Vidal, then bishop designate of Sierra Leone,[1] "is designed to give expression to thought. Hence, by examining the particular class of composition"—and, I may add, the grammatical and syntactical niceties characterizing that composition—"to which any given dialect has been especially devoted, we may trace the direction in which the current of thought is wont to flow amongst the tribe or nations in which it is vernacular, and so investigate the principal psychical peculiarities, if such there be, of that tribe or nation." And

---

[1] "Introductory Remarks to a Vocabulary of the Yoruba Language." Seeleys, Fleet Street, London.

again he remarks: "Dr. Krap was unable to find any word expressing the idea of gratitude in the language of all the Suaheli (Wásawahíli) tribes; a fact significant enough as to the total absence of the moral feeling denoted by that name." Similarly the Mpongwe cannot express our "honesty;" they must paraphrase it by "good man don't steal." In time they possibly may adopt the word bodily like pús (a cat), amog (mug), kapinde (carpenter), krus (a cross), and ilepot (pot).

Such a task is difficult as it is interesting, the main obstacle to success being the almost insuperable difficulty of throwing off European ideas and modes of thought, which life-long habit has made a second nature. Take the instance borrowed from Dr. Krap, and noticed by a hundred writers, namely, the absence of a synonym for "gratitude" amongst the people of the nearer East. I have explained the truth of the case in my "Pilgrimage," and it will bear explanation again. The Wásawahíli are Moslems, and the Moslem view everywhere is that the donor's Maker, not the donor, gives the gift. The Arab therefore expresses his "Thank you!" by "Mamnún"—I am under an obligation (to your hand which has passed on the donation); he generally prefers, however, a short blessing, as "Kassir khayr' ak" (may Allah) "increase thy weal!" The Persian's "May thy shadow never be less!" simply refers to the shade which you, the towering tree, extend over him, the humble shrub.

Another instance of deduction distorted by current European ideas, is where Casalis ("Études sur la langue Séchuana," par Eugène Casalis, part ii. p. 84), speaking of the Sisuto proverbs, makes them display the "vestiges of that universal conscience to which the Creator has committed the guidance of every intelligent creature." Surely it is time to face the fact that conscience is a purely geographical and chronological accident. Where, may we ask, can be that innate and universal monitor in the case of a people, the Somal for instance, who rob like Spartans, holding theft a virtue; who lie like Trojans, without a vestige of appreciation for truth; and who hold the treacherous and cowardly murder of a sleeping guest to be the height of human honour? And what easier than to prove that there is no sin however infamous, no crime however abominable, which at some time or in some part of the world has been or is still held in the highest esteem? The utmost we can say is that conscience, the accident, flows directly from an essential. All races now known to the world have a something which they call right, and a something which they term wrong; the underlying instinctive idea being evidently that everything which benefits me is good, and all which harms me is evil. Their good and their evil are not those of more advanced nations; still the idea is there, and progress or tradition works it out in a thousand different ways.

My visits to Mr. Walker first gave me the idea of making the negro describe his own character in a collection of purely Hamitic proverbs and idioms. It appeared to me that, if ever a book aspires to the title of "*l'Africain peint par lui-même*," it must be one in which he is the medium to his own spirit, the interpreter to his own thoughts. Hence "Wit and Wisdom from West Africa" (London, Tinsleys, 1856), which I still hold to be a step in the right direction, although critics, who possibly knew more of Cornhill than of Yoruba, assured me that it was "rather a heavy compilation." Nor can I yet see how the light fantastic toe can show its agility in the *sabots* of African proverbs.

CHAPTER VIII.

UP THE GABOON RIVER.

DETESTABLE weather detained me long at the hospitable factory. Tornadoes were of almost daily occurrence —not pleasant with 200 barrels of gunpowder under a thatched roof; they were useful chiefly to the Mpongwe servants of the establishment. These model thieves broke open, under cover of the storms, a strong iron safe in an inner room which had been carefully closed; they stole my Mboko skin, and bottles were not safe from them even in our bedrooms.

My next step was to ascend the "Olo' Mpongwe," or Gaboon River, which Bowdich ("Sketch of Gaboon") calls Oroöngo, and its main point Ohlombopolo. The object was to visit the Fá*n*, of whose cannibalism such curious tales had been told. It was not easy to find a conveyance. The factory greatly wanted a flat-bottom iron steamer, a stern-wheeler, with sliding keel, and furnaces fit for burning half-dried wood—a craft of fourteen tons, costing perhaps £14 per ton, would be ample in point of size, and would save not a little money to the trader. I was at last fortunate in securing the "Eliza," belonging to Messrs. Hatton and Cookson. She was a fore-and-aft schooner of twenty tons, measuring 42 feet 6 inches over all and put up at Bonny Town by Captain Birkett. She had two masts, and oars in case of calms; her crew was of six hands, including one Fernando, a Congoese, who could actually box the compass. No outfit was this time necessary, beyond a letter to Mr. Tippet, who had charge of the highest establishments up stream. His business consisted chiefly of importing arms, ammunition, and beads of different sorts, especially the red porcelain, locally called Loangos.

On April 10, a little before noon, I set out, despite thunder and lightning, rain, sun, torrential showers, and the vehemently expressed distaste of my crew. The view of the right bank was no longer from afar; it differs in shape and material from the southern, but the distinction appears to me superficial, not extending to the interiors. Off Konig Island we found nine fathoms of water, and wanted them during a bad storm from the south-east; it prevented my landing and inspecting the old Dutch guns, which Bowdich says are remains of the Portuguese. Both this and Parrot Island, lying some five miles south by west, are masses of cocoas, fringed with mangroves; a great contrast with the *prairillon* of the neighbouring Point Ovindo. At last, worn out by a four-knot current and a squall in our teeth, we anchored in four fathoms, about five miles south-east of Konig.

From this point we could easily see the wide gape of the Rembwe, the south-eastern influent, or rather fork, of the Gaboon, which rises in the south-western versant of some meridional chain, and which I was assured can be ascended in three tides. The people told me when too late of a great cavity or sink, which they called Wonga-Wonga; Bowdich represents it to be an "uninhabited savannah of three days' extent, between Empoöngwa and Adjoomba (Mayumba). I saw nothing of the glittering diamond mountains, lying eastward of Wonga-Wonga, concerning which the old traveller was compelled to admit that, "when there was no moon, a pale but distinct light was invariably reflected from a mountain in that quarter, and from no other." It has now died out—this superstition, which corresponds with the carbuncle of Hoy and others of our Scoto-Scandinavian islands.

Resuming our cruize on the next day, we passed on the right a village of "bad Bákele," which had been blown down by the French during the last year; in this little business the "king" and two lieges had been killed. The tribe is large and important, scattered over several degrees north and south of the equator, as is proved by their slaves being collected from distances of several weeks and even months. In 1854 Mr. Wilson numbered them at 100,000. According to local experts they began to press down stream about 1830, driven *à tergo* by their neighbours, the Mpángwe (Fá*n*), even as they themselves are driving the Mpongwes. But they are evidently the Kaylee or Kalay of Bowdich (p. 427), whose capital, "Samashialee," was "the residence of the king, Ohmbay." He places them in their present habitat, and makes them the worst of cannibals. Whilst the "Sheekans" (Shekyani) buried their dead under the bed within the house, these detestable Kaylees ate not only their prisoners, but their defunct friends, whose bodies were "bid for directly the breath was out of them;" indeed, fathers were frequently seen to devour their own children. Bowdich evidently speaks from hearsay; but the Brazil has preserved the old traditions of cannibalism amongst the Gabões.

The Bákele appeared to me very like the coast tribes, only somewhat lighter-coloured and wilder in look, whilst they again are darker-skinned than their eastern neighbours from the inner highlands. Their women are not so well dressed as the "ladies" of the Mpongwe, the chignon is smaller, and there are fewer brass rings. The men, who still cling to the old habit of hunting, cultivate the soil, practise the ruder mechanical arts, and trade with the usual readiness and greed; they asked us a leaf of tobacco for an egg, and four leaves for a bunch of bananas. Missionaries, who, like Messrs. Preston and Best, resided amongst them for years, have observed that, though a mild and timid people, they are ever involved in quarrels with their neighbours. I can hardly understand how they "bear some resemblance to the dwarfish Dokos of the eastern coast," seeing that the latter do not exist.

The Dikele grammar proves the language, which is most closely allied to the Benga dialect, to be one of the great South African family, variously called Kafir, because first studied amongst these people; Ethiopic (very vague), and Nilotic because its great fluvial basin is the Zambezi, not the Nile. As might be expected amongst isolated races, the tongue, though clearly related to that of the Mpongwe and the Mpángwe, has many salient points of difference; for instance, the liquid "r" is wholly wanting. According to Mr. T. Leighton Wilson, perhaps one word in two is the same, or obviously from the same root; consequently verbal resemblances are by no means striking. The orthography of the two differs materially, and in this respect Dikele more resembles the languages of the eastern coast than its western neighbour, at the same time less than the Fiote or the Congoese. It has a larger number of declensions, and its adjectives and pronouns are more flexible and complicated. On the other hand, it possesses few of the conjugations which form so conspicuous a feature in the tongues of the Lower River, and, reversing the usage of the Mpongwe, it makes very little use of the passive.

Running the gauntlet of cheer and chaff from the noisy inmates of the many Bákele villages, and worried by mangrove-flies, we held our way up the muddy and rapidly narrowing stream, whose avenues of rhizophoras and palms acted as windsails; when the breeze failed the sensation was stifling. Lyámbá (*Cannabis sativa*) grew in patches upon the banks, now apparently wild, like that about Lagos and Badagry. Not till evening did the tide serve, enabling us to send our papers for *visa* on board the guard-ship "L'Oise," where a party of young Frenchmen were preparing for *la chasse*. A little higher up stream are two islets, Nenge Mbwendi, so called from its owner, and Nenge Sika, or the Isle of Gold. The Mpongwe all know this name for the precious metal, and the Bákele appear to ignore it: curious to say, it is the Fante and Mandenga word, probably derived from the Arabic Sikkah, which gave rise to the Italian Zecca (mint) and Zecchino. It may have been introduced by the Laptots or Lascar sailors of the Senegal. M. du Chaillu ("Second Expedition," chap. iii.) mentions "the island Nengué Shika" on the Lower Fernão Vaz River; and Bowdich turns the two into Ompoöngu and Soombeä. The third is Anenga-nenga, not Ninga-ninga, about one mile long from north to south, and well wooded with bush and palms; here the Gaboon Mission has a neat building on piles. The senior native *employé* was at Glass Town, and his junior, a youth about nineteen, stood *à la Napoléon* in the doorway, evidently monarch of all he surveyed. I found there one of the Ndiva, the old tribe of Pongo-land, which by this time has probably died out. We anchored off Wosuku, a village of some fifty houses, forming one main street, disposed north-east—south-west, or nearly at right angles with the river. The entrance was guarded by a sentinel and gun, and the "king," Imondo, lay right royally on his belly. A fine plantation of bananas divides the settlement, and the background is dense bush, in which they say "Nyáre" and deer abound. The Bákele supply sheep and fowls to the Plateau, and their main industry consists in dressing plantain-fibre for thread and nets.

We now reach the confluence of the Nkomo or north-eastern, with the Mbokwe, or eastern branch, which anastomose to form the Gaboon; the latter, being apparently the larger of the two, preserves the title Mpolo. Both still require exploration; my friend M. Braouezzec, Lieutenant de Vaisseau, who made charts of the lower bed, utterly failed to make the sources; and the Rev. Mr. Preston, who lived seven months in the interior, could not ascend far. Mr. W. Winwood Reade reached in May, 1862, the rapids of the Nkomo River, but sore feet prevented his climbing the mountain, which he estimates at 2,000 feet, or of tracing the stream to its fountain. Mr. R. B. N. Walker also ascended the Nkomo for some thirty miles, and found it still a large bed with two fathoms of water in the Cacimbo or "Middle dries." In M. du Chaillu's map the Upper Nkomo is a dotted line; according to all authorities, upon the higher and the lower river his direction is too far to the north-east. The good Tippet declares that he once canoed three miles up the Mbokwe, and then marched eastward for five days, covering a hundred miles—which is impossible. He found a line of detached hills, and an elevation where the dews were exceedingly cold; looking towards the utterly unknown Orient, he could see nothing but a thick forest unbroken by streams. He heard from the country people traditions of a Great Lake, which may be that placed by Tuckey in north latitude 2°—3°. The best seasons for travel are said to be March and November, before and after the rains, which swell the water twelve feet.

About Anenge-nenge we could easily see the sub-ranges of the great Eastern Ghats, some twenty miles to the north-east. Here the shallows and the banks projecting from different points made the channel dangerous. Entering the Mbokwe branch we were compelled to use sweeps, or the schooner would have been dashed against the sides; as we learned by the trees, the tides raise the surface two to three feet high. After the third hour we passed the "Fá*n* Komba Vina," or village of King Vina. It stood in a pretty little bay, and the river, some 400 feet broad, was fronted, as is often the case, by the "palaver tree," a glorious Ceiba or bombax. All the people flocked out to enjoy the sight, and my unpractised eye could not distinguish them from Bákele. Above it, also on the right bank, is the now-deserted site where Messrs. Adams and Preston nearly came to grief for bewitching the population with "bad book."

Five slow hours from Anenge-nenge finally placed us, about sunset, at Mayyá*n*, or Tippet Town. The depôt lies a little above the confluence of the Mbokwe and the Londo, or south-eastern fork of the latter. A drunken pilot and a dark and moonless night, with the tide still running in, delayed us till I could hardly distinguish the sable human masses which gathered upon the Styx-like stream to welcome their new Matyem—merchant or white man. Before landing, all the guns on board the steamer were double-loaded and discharged, at the instance of our host, who very properly insisted upon this act of African courtesy—"it would be shame not to fire salute." We were answered by the loudest howls, and by the town muskets, which must have carried the charges of old chambers. Mr. Tippet, an intelligent coloured man from the States, who has been living thirteen years on the Gaboon, since the age of fourteen, and who acts as native trader to Mr. R. B. N. Walker, for ivory, ebony, rubber, and other produce, escorted me to his extensive establishment. At length I am amongst the maneaters.

CHAPTER IX.

A SPECIMEN DAY WITH THE FÁN CANNIBALS.

T 5 a.m. on the next day, after a night with the gnats and rats, I sallied forth in the thick "smokes," and cast a nearer look upon my cannibal hosts. And first of the tribal name. The Mpongwe call their wild neighbours Mpángwe; the Europeans affect such corruptions as Fánwe, Panwe, the F and P being very similar, Phaouin and Paouen (Pawen). They call themselves Fá*n*, meaning "man;" in the plural, Báfa*n*. The *n* is highly nasalized: the missionaries proposed to express it by "*nh*," which, however, wrongly conveys the idea of aspiration; and "Fan," pronounced after the English fashion, would be unintelligible to them.

The village contains some 400 souls, and throughout the country the maximum would be about 500 spears, or 4,000 of both sexes, whilst the minimum is a couple of dozen. It is pleasantly situated on the left bank of the Mbokwe River, a streamlet here some 50 feet broad, whose water rises 6 feet 10 inches under the tidal influence. The single street, about half a mile long, is formed by two parallel rows of huts, looking upon a cleared line of yellow clay, and provided with three larger sheds—the palaver houses. The Fá*n* houses resemble those of the Mpongwe; in fact, the tribes, beginning at the Camarones River, build in much the same style, but all are by no means so neat and clean as those of the seaboard. A thatch, whose projecting eaves form deep shady verandahs, surmounts walls of split bamboo, supported by raised platforms of tamped earth, windows being absent and chimneys unknown; the ceiling is painted like coal tar by oily soot, and two opposite doors make the home a passage through which no one hesitates to pass. The walls are garnished with weapons and nets, both skilfully made, and the furniture consists of cooking utensils and water-pots, mats for bedding, logs of wood for seats and pillows, and lumps of timber or dwarf stools, neatly cut out of a single block. Their only night-light—that grand test of civilization—is the Mpongwe torch, a yard of hard, black gum, mixed with and tightly bound up in dried banana leaves. According to some it is acacia; others declare it to be the "blood" of the bombax, which is also used for caulking. They gather it in the forest, especially during the dries, collect it in hollow bamboos, and prepare it by heating in the neptune, or brass pan. The odour is pleasant, but fragments of falling fire endanger the hut, and trimming must be repeated every ten minutes. The sexes are not separated; as throughout intertropical Africa, the men are fond of idling at their clubs; and the women, who must fetch water and cook, clean the hut, and nurse the baby, are seldom allowed to waste time. They are naturally a more prolific race than those inhabiting the damp, unhealthy lowlands, and the number of the children contrasts pleasantly with the "bleak house" of the debauched Mpongwe, who puts no question when his wife presents him with issue.

In the cool of the morning Fitevanga, king of Mayyá*n*, lectured me upon the short and simple annals of the Fá*n*. In 1842 the first stragglers who had crossed the Sierra del Crystal are said to have been seen upon the head waters of the Gaboon. I cannot, however, but suspect that they are the "Paämways" of whom Bowdich ("Sketch of Gaboon," p. 429) wrote in the beginning of the century, "All the natives on this route are said to be cannibals, the Paämways not so voraciously as the others, because they cultivate a large breed of dogs for their eating." Mr. W. Winwood Reade suspects them to be an offshoot of the great Fulah race, and there is nothing in point of dialect to disprove what we must at present consider a pure conjecture. "The Fulah pronouns have striking analogies with those of the Yoruba, Accra, Ashantee, and Timmanee, and even of the great Kaffir class of dialects, which reaches from the equator to the Cape," wrote the late learned E. Norris, in his "Introduction to the Grammar of the Fulah Language" (London: Harrison, 1854).

According to the people of the upper river the Fá*n* were expelled by the Bati or Batti—not "Bari" as it has been written—from their ancient seats; and they are still pushing them seawards. The bushmen are said to live seven to ten short marches (seventy to a hundred miles) to the east, and are described by Mr. Tippet, whom they have visited, as a fine, tall, slender, and light-skinned people, who dress like the Fá*n*, but without so much clothing, and who sharpen the teeth of both sexes. Dr. Barth heard of the Bati, and Herr Petermann's map describes them[1] as "Pagans, reported to be of a white colour, and of beautiful shape, to live in houses made of clay, to wear cloth of their own making, and to hold a country from which a mountain is visible to the south-west, and close to the sea." The range in question may be the Long Qua (Kwa), which continues the Camarones block to the north-east, and the Batis may have passed south-westward from Southern Adamáwa.

---

[1] Hutchinson's "Ten Years' Wanderings," p. 319.

The F*án* were accompanied in their seaward movement by the Osheba or 'Sheba, the Moshebo and Moshobo of M. du Chaillu's map. They are said to be a tribe of kindred blood and warlike tastes, speaking a remarkably guttural tongue, but intelligible to the Mpángwe. They too were doubtless pressed forward by the Inner Bati, who are also affected by the Okáná, the Yefá, and the Sensobá. The latter are the innermost known to my negro informants, and their sheep and goats have found their way to the Gaboon: they are doughty elephant-hunters, and they attack the Njína, although they have no fire-arms. The Mpángwe deride the savagery of these races, who have never heard of a man riding a horse or an ass, which the Mpongwes call Cavala and Buro burro). The names of these three races, which are described as brave, warlike, and hospitable to strangers, will not be found on any map; indeed the regions east of the Gaboon belong to the great white blot of inter-tropical Africa, extending from north latitude 7° to south latitude 5°. Major de Ruvignes heard also of a tribe called Lachaize (Osheba?) which excels the F*án* in strength and courage as much as the latter do the coast tribes: a detachment of them had settled near one of the chief Mpángwe towns, "Mboma." Some days after his arrival he saw several of these people, and describes them as giants, compared with the negro races to which his eye was accustomed. The general stature varied from six feet to six feet four inches; their complexion was a light *café au lait;* their hair was ornamented with cowries, strung so thickly as to suggest a skull-cup, whilst long streamers of elephants' tails, threaded with the Cypræa and brass rings, hung down from the head behind the ears, covering the nape of the neck. All these, we may observe, are Congo customs. In their manufacture of iron, dug by themselves, they resemble the cannibals.

The Fá*n* have now lodged themselves amongst the less warlike, maritime, and sub-maritime tribes, as the (Ashantis) Asiante lately did in Fante-land; now they visit the factories on the estuary, and wander as far as the Ogobe. In course of time, they will infallibly "eat up" the Bákele, as the latter are eating up the Mpongwe and Shekyani. They have their own names for neighbouring tribes: the Mpongwe, according to Bowdich, called the Shekyani, and the inner tribes "Boolas, a synonym of Dunko in Ashantee;" hence, probably, the "Bulous" of Mr. Hutchinson (p. 253), "a tribe on the Guergay Creek, who speak a different language from the Mpongwes." The Fá*n* call the Mpongwes, Báyok; the Bákele, Ngo*n*; the Shekyani, Besek; and the Gaboon River, Aboka. The sub-tribes of cannibals, living near my line of march, were named to me as follows:—1. The

Lálá (Oshebas ?), whose chief settlement, Sánkwí, is up the Mbokwe River; 2. their neighbours, the Esánvímá; 3. the Sánikiya, a bush tribe; 4. the Sákulá, near Mayyá*n*; 5. the Esobá, about Fakanjok; 6. the Esonzel of the Ute, or Autá village; 7. the Okola, whose chief settlement is Esámási; and 8. the Ashemvon, with Asya for a capital.

From M. du Chaillu's illustrations (pp. 74, 77) I fully expected to see a large-limbed, black-skinned, and ferocious-looking race, with huge mustachios and plaited beards. A finely made, light-coloured people, of regular features and decidedly mild aspect, met my sight.

The complexion is, as a rule, chocolate, the distinctive colour of the African mountaineer and of the inner tribes; there are dark men, as there would be in England, but the very black are of servile origin. Few had any signs of skin-disease; I saw only one hand spotted with white, like the incipient Morphetico (leper) of the Brazil. Many, if bleached, might pass for Europeans, so "Caucasian" are their features; few are negro in type as the Mpongwe, and none are purely "nigger" like the blacks of maritime Guinea and the lower Congoese. And they bear the aspect of a people fresh from the bush, the backwoods; their teeth are pointed, and there is generally a look of grotesqueness and surprise. When I drank tea, they asked what was the good of putting sugar in tobacco water. The hair is not kinky, pepper-corn-like, and crisply woolly, like that of the Coast tribes; in men, as well as in women, it falls in a thick curtain, nearly to the shoulders, and it is finer than the usual elliptical fuzz. The variety of their perruquerie can be rivalled only by that of the dress and ornament. The males affect plaits, knobs, and horns, stiff twists and upright tufts, suddenly projecting some two inches from the scalp; and, that analogies with Europe might not be wanting, one gentleman wore a queue, *zopf*, or pigtail, bound at the shoulders, not by a ribbon, but by the neck of a claret bottle. Other heads are adorned with single feathers, or bunches and circles of plumes, especially the red tail-plumes of the parrot and the crimson coat of the Touraco (Corythrix), an African jay; these blood-coloured spoils are a sign of war. The Brazilian traveller will be surprised to find the coronals of feathers, the Kennitare (Acangátara) of the Tupí-Guaraní race, which one always associates with the New World. The skull-caps of plaited and blackened palm leaf, though common in the interior, are here rare; an imitation is produced by tressing the hair longitudinally from occiput to sinciput, making the head a system of ridges, divided by scalp-lines, and a fan-shaped tuft of scarlet-stained palm frond surmounts the poll. I noticed a fashion of crinal decoration quite new to me.

A few hairs, either from the temples, the sides or the back of the head, are lengthened with tree-fibres, and threaded with red and white pound-beads, so called by Europeans because the lb. fetches a dollar. These decorations fall upon the breast or back; the same is done to the thin beard, which sprouts tufty from both rami of the chin, as in the purely nervous temperament of

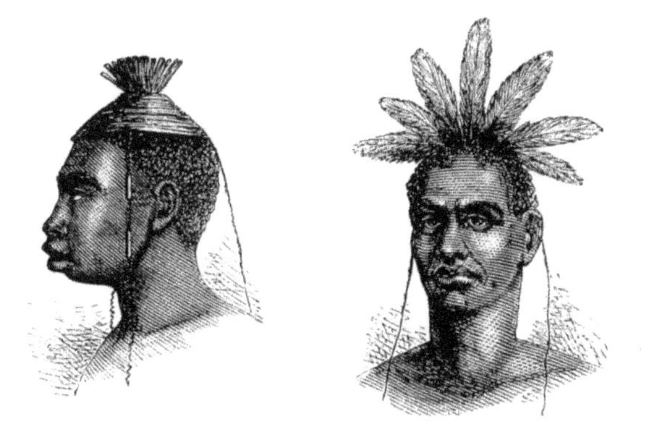

FÁN HEAD-DRESS.

Europe; and doubtless the mustachios, if the latter were not mostly wanting, would be similarly treated. Whatever absurdity in hair may be demanded by the trichotomists and philopogons of Europe, I can at once supply it to any extent from Africa—gratis. Gentlemen remarkable by a *raie*, which as in the Scotch terrier begins above the eyes and runs down the back, should be grateful to me for this sporting offer.

Nothing simpler than the Fá*n* toilette. Thongs and plaits of goat, wild cat, or leopard skin gird the waist, and cloth, which is rare, is supplied by the spoils of the black monkey or some other "beef." The main part of the national costume, and certainly the most remarkable, is a fan of palm frond redolent of grease and ruddled with ochre, thrust through the waist belt; while new and stiff the upper half stands bolt upright and depends only when old. It suggests the "Enduap" (rondache) of ostrich-plumes worn by the Tupí-Guaraní barbarians of the Brazil, the bunchy caudal appendages which made the missionaries compare them with pigeons. The fore part of the body is here decked with a similar fan, the outspread portion worn the wrong way, like that behind. The ornaments are seed-beads, green or white, and Loangos (red porcelain). The "bunch" here contains 100 to 120 strings, and up country 200, worth one dollar; each will weigh from one to three, and a wealthy Fá*n* may carry fifteen to forty-five pounds. The seed-bead was till lately unknown; fifteen to twenty strings make the "bunch." There is not much tattooing amongst the men, except on the shoulders, whilst the women prefer the stomach; the *gandin*, however, disfigures himself with powdered cam-wood, mixed with butter-nut, grease, or palm oil—a custom evidently derived from the coast-tribes. Each has his "Ndese," garters and armlets of plaited palm fibre, and tightened by little cross-bars of brass; they are the "Hibás" which the Bedawin wear under their lower articulations as preservatives against cramp. Lastly, a Fetish horn hangs from the breast, and heavy copper rings encumber the wrists and ankles. Though unskilful in managing canoes—an art to be learned, like riding and dancing, only in childhood—many villagers affect to walk about with a paddle, like the semi-aquatic Kru-men. Up country it is said they make rafts which are towed across the stream by ropes, when the swiftness of the current demands a ferry. The women are still afraid of the canoe.

All adult males carry arms, and would be held womanish if they were seen unweaponed. These are generally battle-axes, spears cruelly and fantastically jagged, hooked and barbed, and curious leaf-shaped knives of archaic aspect; some of the latter have blades broader than they are long, a shape also preserved by the Mpongwe. The sheaths of fibre or leather are elaborately decorated, and it is *chic* for the scabbard to fit so tight that the weapon cannot be drawn for five minutes; I have seen the same amongst the Somal. There are some trade-muskets, but the "hot-mouthed weapon" has not become the national weapon of the Fá*n*. Bows and arrows are unknown; the Náyin or cross-bow peculiar to this people, and probably a native invention, not borrowed, as might be supposed, from Europe, is carried only when hunting or fighting: a specimen was exhibited in London with the gorillas. The people are said sometimes to bend it with the foot or feet like the Tupí Guaranís, the Jivaros, and other South Americans. Suffice it to remark of this weapon, with which, by the by, I never saw a decent shot made, that the *détente* is simple and ingenious, and that the "Ebe" or dwarf bolt is always poisoned with the boiled root of a wild shrub. It is believed that a graze is fatal, and that the death is exceedingly painful: I doubt both assertions. Most men also carry a pliable basket full of bamboo caltrops, thin splints, pointed and poisoned. Placed upon the path of a bare-footed enemy, this rude contrivance, combined with the scratching of the thorns, and the gashing cuts of the grass, must somewhat discourage pursuit. The shields of elephant hide are large, square, and ponderous. The "terrible war-axe" is the usual poor little tomahawk, more like a toy than a tool.

After a bathe in the muddy Mbokwe, I returned to the village, and found it in a state of ferment. The Fá*n*, like all inner African tribes, with whom fighting is our fox-hunting, live in a chronic state of ten days' war, and can never hold themselves safe; this is the case especially where the slave trade has never been heard of. Similarly the Ghazwah (" Razzia") of the Bedawin is for plunder, not for captives. Surprises are rare, because they will not march in the dark. Battles are not bloody; after two or three warriors have fallen their corpses

FÁN WARRIOR.

are dragged away to be devoured, their friends save themselves by flight, and the weaker side secures peace by paying sheep and goats. On this occasion the sister of a young "brave" had just now been killed and "chopped" by the king of Sánkwí, a neighbouring settlement of Oshebas, and the bereaved brother was urging his comrades with vociferous speeches to "up and arm." Usually when a man wants "war," he rushes naked through his own village, cursing it as he goes. Moreover, during the last war Mayyá*n* lost five men to three of the enemy; which is not fair, said the women, who appeared most eager for the fray. All the youths seized their weapons; the huge war-drums, the hollowed bole of a tree fringed with Nyáre hide, was set up in the middle of the street; preparations for the week of singing and dancing which precedes a campaign were already in hand, and one war-man gave earnest of bloodshed by spearing a goat the property of Mr. Tippet. It being our interest that the peace should be kept till after my proposed trip into the interior, I repaired to the palaver-house and lent weight to the advice of my host, who urged the heroes to collect ivory, ebony, and rubber, and not to fight till his stores were filled. We concluded by carrying off the goat. After great excitement the warriors subsided to a calm; it was broken, however, two days afterwards by the murder of a villager, the suspected lover of a woman whose house was higher up the Mbokwe River; he went to visit her, and was incontinently speared in the breast by the "injured husband." If he die and no fine be paid, there will be another "war."

I made careful inquiry about anthropophagy.

amongst the Fá*n*, and my account must differ greatly from that of M. du Chaillu. The reader, however, will remember that Mayyá*n* is held by a comparatively civilized race, who have probably learned to conceal a custom so distasteful to all their neighbours, white and black; in the remoter districts cannibalism may yet assume far more hideous proportions. Since the Fá*n* have encouraged traders to settle amongst them, the interest

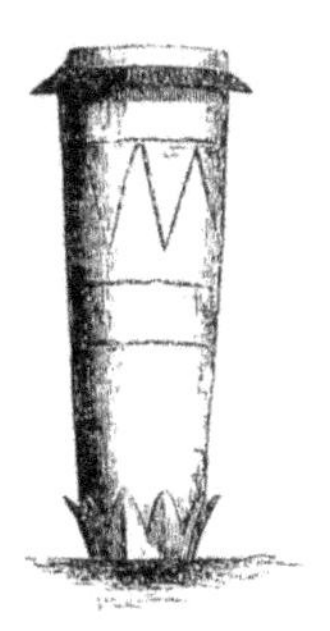

THE DRUM.

as well as the terrors of the Coast tribes, who would deter foreigners from direct dealings, has added new horrors to the tale; and yet nothing can exceed the reports of older travellers.

During my peregrinations I did not see a single skull. The chiefs, stretched at full length, and wrapped in mats, are buried secretly, the object being to prevent some strong Fetish medicine being made by enemies from various parts of the body.

In some villages the head men of the same tribe are interred near one another; the commonalty are put singly and decently under ground, and only the slave (Máká) is thrown as usual into the bush. Mr. Tippet, who had lived three years with this people, knew only three cases of cannibalism; and the Rev. Mr. Walker agreed with other excellent authorities, that it is a rare incident even in the wildest parts—perhaps opportunity only is wanted. As will appear from the Fá*n*'s bill of fare, anthropophagy can hardly be caused by necessity, and the way in which it is conducted shows that it is a quasi-religious rite practised upon foes slain in battle, evidently an equivalent of human sacrifice. If the whole body cannot be carried off, a limb or two is removed for the purpose of a roast. The corpse is carried to a hut built expressly on the outskirts of the settlement; it is eaten secretly by the warriors, women and children not being allowed to be present, or even to look upon man's flesh; and the cooking pots used for the banquet must all be broken. A joint of "black brother" is never seen in the villages: "smoked human flesh" does not hang from the rafters, and the leather knife-sheaths are of wild cow; tanned man's skin suggests only the *tannerie de Meudon*, an advanced "institution." Yet Dr. Schweinfurth's valuable travels on the Western Nile prove that public anthropophagy can co-exist with a considerable amount of comfort and, so to speak, civilization—witness the Nyam-Nyam and Mombattu (Mimbut-too). The sick and the dead are uneaten by the Fá*n*, and the people shouted with laughter when I asked a certain question.

The "unnatural" practice, which, by the by, has at different ages extended over the whole world,

THE CANNIBAL.

now continues to be most prevalent in places where, as in New Zealand, animal food is wanting; and everywhere pork readily takes the place of "long pig." The damp and depressing atmosphere of equatorial Africa renders the stimulus of flesh diet necessary. The Isángú, or Ingwánba, the craving felt after a short abstinence from animal food, does not spare the white traveller more than it does his dark guides; and, though the moral courage of the former may resist the "gastronomic practice" of breaking fast upon a fat young slave, one does not expect so much from the untutored appetite of the noble savage. On the eastern parts of the continent there are two cannibal tribes, the Wadoe and the Wabembe; and it is curious to find the former occupying the position assigned by Ptolemy (iv. 8) to his anthropophagi of the *Barbaricus Sinus:* according to their own account, however, the practice is modern. When weakened by the attacks of their Wákámbá neighbours, they began to roast and eat slices from the bodies of the slain in presence of the foe. The latter, as often happens amongst barbarians, and even amongst civilized men, could dare to die, but were unable to face the horrors of becoming food after death: the great Cortez knew this feeling when he made his soldiers pretend anthropophagy. Many of the Wadoe negroids are tall, well made, and light complexioned, though inhabiting the low and humid coast regions—a proof, if any were wanted, that there is nothing unwholesome in man's flesh. Some of our old accounts of shipwrecked seamen, driven to the dire necessity of eating one another, insinuate that the impious food causes raging insanity. The Wabembe tribe, occupying a strip of land on the western shore of the Tanganyika

Lake, are "Menschenfresser," as they were rightly called by the authors of the "Mombas Mission Map." These miserables have abandoned to wild growth a most prolific soil; too lazy and unenergetic to hunt or to fish, they devour all manner of carrion, grubs, insects, and even the corpses of their deceased friends. The Midgán, or slave-caste of the semi-Semitic Somal, are sometimes reduced to the same extremity; but they are ever held, like the Wendigo, or man-eaters, amongst the North American Indians, impure and detestable. On the other hand, the Tupí-Guaranís of the Brazil, a country abounding in game, fish, wild fruits, and vegetables, ate one another with a surprising relish. This subject is too extensive even to be outlined here: the reader is referred to the translation of Hans Stade: old travellers attribute the cannibalism of the Brazilian races to "gulosity" rather than superstition; moreover, these barbarians had certain abominable practices, supposed to be known only to the most advanced races.

Anthropophagy without apparent cause was not unknown in Southern Africa. Mr. Layland found a tribe of "cave cannibals" amongst the mountains beyond Thaba Bosigo in the Trans-Gariep Country.[1] He remarks with some surprise,

---

[1] "Journal of the Ethnological Society," April, 1869.

" Horrible as all this may appear, there might be some excuse made for savages, driven by famine to extreme hunger, for capturing and devouring their enemies. But with these people it was totally different, for they were inhabiting a fine agricultural tract of country, which also abounded in game. Notwithstanding this, they were not contented with hunting and feeding upon their enemies, but preyed much upon each other also, for many of their captures were made from amongst the people of their own tribe, and, even worse than this, in times of scarcity, many of their own wives and children became the victims of this horrible practice."

Anthropophagy, either as a necessity, a sentiment, or a superstition, is known to sundry, though by no means to all, the tribes dwelling between the Nun (Niger) and the Congo rivers; how much farther south it extends I cannot at present say. On the Lower Niger, and its branch the Brass River, the people hardly take the trouble to conceal it. On the Bonny and New Calabar, perhaps the most advanced of the so-called Oil Rivers, cannibalism, based upon a desire of revenge, and perhaps, its sentimental side, the object of imbibing the valour of an enemy slain in battle, has caused many scandals of late years. The practice, on the other hand, is execrated by the Efiks of Old Calabar, who punish any attempts of the kind with extreme severity. During 1862 the slaves of Creek-town attempted it, and were killed. At Duke-town an Ibo woman also cut up a man, sun-dried the flesh, and sold it for monkey's meat—she took sanctuary at the mission house. Yet it is in full vigour amongst their Ibo neighbours to the north-west, and the Duallas of the Camarones River also number it amongst their "country customs." The Mpongwe, as has been said, will not eat a chimpanzee; the Fá*n* devour their dead enemies.

The Fá*n* character has its ferocious side, or it would not be African: prisoners are tortured with all the horrible barbarity of that human wild beast which is happily being extirpated, the North American Indian; and children may be seen greedily licking the blood from the ground. It is a curious ethnological study, this peculiar development of destructiveness in the African brain. Cruelty seems to be with him a necessary of life, and all his highest enjoyments are connected with causing pain and inflicting death. His religious rites—a strong contrast to those of the modern Hindoo—are ever causelessly bloody. Take as an instance, the Efik race, or people of Old Calabar, some 6,000 wretched remnants of a once-powerful tribe. For 200 years they have had intercourse with Europeans, who, though slavers, would certainly neither enjoy nor encourage these profitless horrors; yet no savages show more brutality in torture, more frenzied delight in bloodshed, than they do. A few of their pleasant practices are—

The administration of Esere, or poison-bean;

"Egbo floggings" of the utmost severity, equalling the knout;

Substitution of an innocent pauper for a rich criminal;

Infanticide of twins; and

Vivisepulture.

And it must be remembered that this tribe has had the benefit of a resident mission for the last generation. I can hardly believe this abnormal cruelty to be the mere result of uncivilization; it appears to me the effect of an arrested development, which leaves to the man all the ferocity of the carnivor, the unreflecting cruelty of the child.

The dietary of these "wild men of the woods" would astonish the starveling sons of civilization. When will the poor man realize the fact that his comfort and happiness will result not from workhouses and almshouses, hospitals and private charities, but from that organized and efficient emigration, so long advocated by the seer Carlyle? Only the crassest ignorance and the listlessness born of misery and want prevent the able-bodied pauper, the frozen-out mechanic, or the weary and ill-clad, the over-worked and underfed agricultural labourer, from quitting the scenes of his purgatory, and from finding, scattered over earth's surface, spots where he may enjoy a comparative paradise, heightened by the memory of privations endured in the wretched hole which he pleases to call his home. But *nostalgia* is a more common disease than men suppose, and it affects none more severely than those that are remarkable for their physical powers. A national system of emigration, to be perfect, must not be confined to solitary and individual hands, who, however numerous, are ever pining for the past. The future will organize the exodus of whole villages, which, like those of the Hebrides in the last century, will bear with them to new worlds their Lares and Penates, their wives, families, and friends, who will lay out the church and the churchyard after the old fashion familiar to their youth, and who will not forget the palaver-house, vulgarly called pothouse or pub.

Few of these Lestrigons lack fish, which they catch in weirs, fowl, flesh of dogs, goats, or sheep; cattle is a luxury yet unknown, but the woods supply an abundance of Nyáre and other "bush-beef." They also have their special word for the meat-yearning. Still in the semi-nomadic stage, they till the ground, and yet depend greatly upon the chase. They break their fast (kidiashe) at 6 A.M., eat a mid-day meal (amos), and sup (gogáshe) at sunset, besides "snacks" all through the day when they can find material. They are good huntsmen, who fear neither the elephant (nyok), the hippopotamus (nyok á mádzim), frequent in the rivers of the interior, the crocodile, nor the gorilla (njí). It is generally asserted—and the unfortunate Douville re-echoed the assertion—that the river-horse and the crocodile will not live together; the reason is, simply, that upon the seaboard, where these animals were first observed, the crocodile prefers the fresh water of the river, the hippopotamus the brackish water at its mouth. In the interior, of course, they dwell together in amity, because there is nothing for them to quarrel about.

The banana, planted with a careless hand, supplies the staff of life, besides thatch, fuel, and fibre for nets and lines: when they want cereals, maize, holcus, and panicum will grow almost spontaneously. The various palm-trees give building materials, oil, wine, and other requisites too numerous to mention. The "five products of the cow" are ignored, as in the western hemisphere of yore: one of the most useful, however, is produced by the Nje or Njeve, a towering butyraceous tree, differing from that which bears the Shea butter-nut. Its produce is sun-dried, toasted over a fire, pounded and pressed in a bag between two boards, when it is ready for use. The bush, cut at the end, is fired before the beginning, of the rains, leaving the land ready for yams and sweet potatoes almost without using the hoe. In the middle dries, from June to September, the villagers sally forth *en masse* for a battue of elephants, whose spoils bring various luxuries from the coast. Lately, before my arrival, they had turned out to gather the Abá, or wild mango, for Odika sauce; and during this season they will do nothing else. The Fá*n* plant their own tobacco, which is described as a low, spreading plant, and despise the imported weed; they neither snuff nor chew. All manufacture their own pipe-bowls, and they are not ignorant of the use of Lyámbá or Hashish. They care little for sugar, contrary to the rule of Africa in general, but they over-salt all their food; and they will suck the condiment as children do lollipops. Their palm oil is very poor, as if they had only just learned the art of making it.

After the daily siesta, which lasted till 3 P.M., Mr. Tippet asked me to put in an appearance at a solemn dance which, led by the king's eldest daughter, was being performed in honour of the white visitor. A chair was placed in the verandah, the street being the ballroom. Received with the usual salutation, "Mboláne," to which the reply is "A*n*," I proceeded to the external study of Fá*n* womanhood. Whilst the men are tall and *élancés*, their partners are usually short and stout, and,

> "Her stature tall, I hate a dumpy woman,"

is a matter of taste upon which most of us agree with his lordship. This peculiar breadth of face and person probably result from hard work and good fare, developing adipose tissue. I could not bring myself to admire Gondebiza, the princess royal,—what is grotesque in one sex becomes unsightly in the other. Fat, thirty, and perhaps once fair, her charms had seen their prime, and the system of circles and circlets which composed her *personnel* had assumed a tremulous and gravitating tendency. She was habited in the height of Fá*n* fashion. Her body was modestly invested in a thin pattern of tattoo, and a gauze-work of oil and camwood; the rest of the toilette was a dwarf pigeon-tail of fan-palm, like that of the men, and a manner of apron, white beads, and tree bark, greasy and reddened: the latter was tucked under and over the five lines of cowries, which acted as cestus to the portly middle, "big as a budget." The horns of hair, not unlike the rays of light in Michael Angelo's "Moses," were covered with a cap of leaves, and they were balanced behind by a pigtail lashed with brass wire. Her ornaments were sundry necklaces of various beads, large red and white, and small blue and pink porcelains; a leaf, probably by way of amulet, was bound to a string round the upper arm; and wrists and ankles were laden with heavy rings of brass and copper, the parure of the great in Fá*n*-land. The other *ballerine* were, of course, less brilliantly attired, but all had rings on their arms, legs, and ankles, fingers, and toes. A common decoration was a bunch of seven or eight long ringlets, not unlike the *queues de rat*, still affected by the old-fashioned Englishwoman; these, however, as in the men, were prolonged to the bosom by strings of alternate red and white beads. Others limited the decoration to two rats' tails depending from the temples, where phrenologists localize our "causality." Many had faces of sufficient piquancy; the figures, though full, wanted firmness, and I noticed only one well-formed bosom. The men wore red feathers, but none carried arms.

The form of saltation suggested Mr. Catlin's drawings. A circular procession of children, as well as adults, first promenaded round the princess, who danced with all her might in the centre, her countenance preserving the *grand sérieux*. The performers in this "ging-a-ring" then clapped hands with prolonged ejaculations of o-o-o-oh, stamped and shuffled forwards, moving the body from the hips downwards, whilst H. R. H. alone stood stationary and smileless as a French demoiselle of the last century, who came to the ball not to *causer* but to *danser*. At times, when King Fitevanga condescended to show his agility, the uproar of applause became deafening. The orchestra consisted of two men sitting opposite each other,—one performed on a caisson, a log of hollowed wood, four feet high, skin-covered, and fancifully carved; the other on the national Anjyá, a rude "Marimba," the prototype of the pianoforte. It is made of seven or eight hard-wood slats, pinned with bamboo tacks to transverse banana trunks lying on the ground: like the *grande caisse*, it is played upon with sticks, plectra like tent-pegs. Mr. W. Winwood Reade ("Savage Africa," chap. xiii.) says: "The instrument is also described by Froebel as being used by the Indians of Central America, where, which is still more curious, it is known by the same name—'marimba.'" Of course they borrowed the article and the name from the negroes: most tribes in Africa have their own terms for this universal instrument, but it is everywhere recognized by the African who knows Europeans as "marimba." Thus Owen tells us (p. 308) "that at the mouth of the Zambesi it is called 'Tabbelah,'" evidently the Arabic "Tablah" Another favourite instrument is a clapper, made of two bamboos some five feet long, and thick as capstan bars,—it is truly the castanet *en grand*.

Highly gratified by the honour, but somewhat overpowered by the presence and by that vile scourge the sandfly, I retired after the first review, leaving the song, the drum, and the dance to continue till midnight. Accustomed to the frantic noises of African village-life in general, my ears here recognized an excess of bawl and shout, and subsequent experience did not efface the impression. But, in the savage and the barbarian, noise, like curiosity, is a healthy sign; the lowest tribes are moping and apathetic as sick children; they will hardly look at anything, however strange to them.

The rest of my day and week was devoted to the study of this quaint people, and the following are the results. Those who have dealings with the Fá*n* universally prefer them in point of honesty and manliness to the Mpongwe and Coast races; they have not had time to become thoroughly corrupt, to lose all the lesser without gaining anything of the greater virtues. They boast, like John Tod, that they ne'er feared the French, and have scant respect for (white) persons; indeed, their independence sometimes takes the form of insolence. We were obliged to release by force the boy Nyongo, and two of Mr. Tippet's women who had been put "in log"—*Anglicè*, in the stocks. They were wanted as hostages during the coming war, and this rude contrivance was adopted to insure their presence.

Chastity is still known amongst the Fá*n*. The

marriage tie has some significance, the women will not go astray except with the husband's leave, which is not often granted. The men wax wroth if their mothers be abused. It is an insult to call one of them a liar or a coward; the coast-tribes would merely smile at the soft impeachment, and assure you that none but fools—yourself included by implication—are anything else. Their bravery is the bravery of the savage, whose first object in battle is to preserve his only good, his life: to the civilized man, therefore, they appear but moderately courageous. They are fond of intoxication, but are not yet broken to ardent spirits: I have seen a single glass of trade rum cause a man to roll upon the ground and convulsively bite the yellow clay like one in the agonies of the death-thirst. They would do wisely to decline intercourse with Europeans; but this, of course, is impossible—there is a manifest destiny for them as for their predecessors. The vile practice of the white or West Coast is to supply savages with alcohol, arms, and ammunition; to live upon the lives of those they serve. The more honourable Moslems of the eastern shores do not disgrace themselves by such greed of gain.

The Fá*n* are cunning workers in iron, which is their wealth. Their money is composed of Ikíá, dwarf bars shaped like horse-fleams, a coinage familiar to old travellers in West Africa, and of this Spartan currency a bundle of ten represents sixpence. "White man's Ikíá" would be silver, for which the more advanced Mpongwe have corrupted the English to "solove." An idea exists on the Lower River that our hardware is broken up for the purpose of being made into spear-heads and other weapons. Such is not generally the case. The Wamasai, the Somal and the Cape Kafirs—indeed, all the metal-working African barbarians—call our best Sheffield blades "rotten iron." They despise a material that chips and snaps, and they prefer with ample cause their native produce, charcoal-smelted, and tempered by many successive heatings and hammerings, without quenching in water. Nor will they readily part with it when worked. The usual trade medium is a metal rod; two of these are worth a franc if of brass, while three of copper represent two francs. There is a great demand for beads and salt, the latter especially throughout the interior.

Thus ended my "first impressions" amongst the Fá*n* cannibals.

CHAPTER X

TO THE MBIKA (HILL); THE SOURCES OF THE GABOON.—RETURN TO THE PLATEAU.

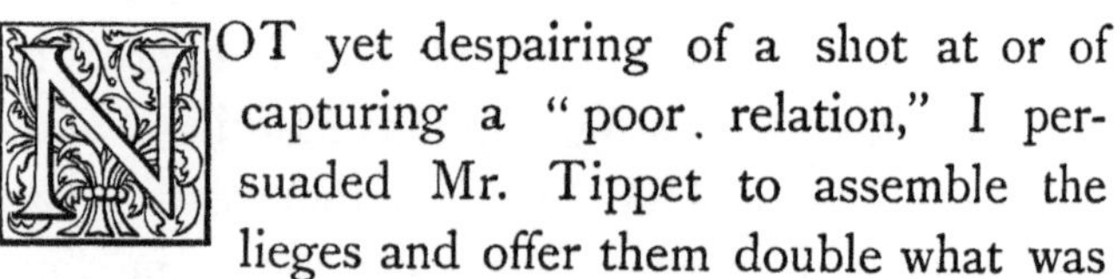

NOT yet despairing of a shot at or of capturing a "poor relation," I persuaded Mr. Tippet to assemble the lieges and offer them double what was proposed at Mbátá. No one, however, appeared sanguine of success, the anthropoid keeps his distance from the Fá*n*. A trip to the interior was suggested, first up the Mbokwe, and finally arranged for the Londo River. Information about the country was, as usual, vague; one man made the stream head two days off, the other a few hours, and Mr. Tippet's mind fluctuated between fifty and one hundred miles.

The party was easily assembled, and we set out at 7 A.M. on April 14th. I and Selim had the dignity of a "dingy" to ourselves: Mr. Tippet out of a little harem of twenty-five had chosen two wives and sundry Abigails; his canoe, laden with some fifteen souls, was nearly flush with the water. The beauties were somewhat surly, they complained, like the sluggard, of too early waking

ANKOMBE.

and swore that they would do nothing in the way of work, industry being essentially servile. Anne Coombe (Ankombe, daughter of Qua-ben), was a short, stout, good-humoured lass; "'Lizer" (Eliza), I regret to say, would not make the least exertion, and, when called, always turned her back.

After dropping three miles down the Mbokwe River, we entered the Londo influent: some three miles further on it fines down from a width of eighty feet to a mere ditch, barred with trees, which stop navigation. We landed on the left bank and walked into the palaver-house of Fakanjok or Pakanjok, the village of a Fá*n* head man, called by Mr. Tippet "John Matoko." It was old, dirty and tattered, showing signs of approaching removal. Out of the crowd of men and women who nearly sat upon us, I had no difficulty in hiring eight porters, thereby increasing our party to twenty-five souls. These people carry on the shoulder, not as Africans always should do, on the head: they even cross the fallen trunks which act as rickety bridges, with one side of the body thus heavier than the other.

The bush-path began by wheeling westward, as though we were returning to Anenge-nenge; thence it struck south-eastwards, a rhumb from which it rarely deviated. Though we were approaching the sub-ranges of the Sierra del Crystal, the country was very like that about Mbátá; streamlets flowing to the Mbokwe, wet yellow soil forming slippery muds, unhealthy as unpleasant in the morning sunshine; old and new clearings and plantations, mostly of bananas, mere spots in the wide expanse of bush, and deserted or half-inhabited villages. Shortly after noon we came to a battle-field, where the heroes of Tippet-town had chanced to fall in with their foes of Autá, a settlement distant eight or nine miles. Both armies at once "tree'd" themselves behind

" 'LIZER."

trunks, and worked at long bowls; the "bush-men," having only one gun and two charges, lost four of their men, and the victors, who had no time to carry off the slain, contented themselves with an arm or two by way of *gigot*.

Probably the memory of this affair, which is still to be settled, unfavourably impressed my escort. After a total of some two hours (six miles) we arrived at a large "Oláko" or break-wind, a half-face of leafy branches, and all insisted upon a long rest. I objected, and then "palaver came up." We were at last frankly told that the villages ahead were hostile, that we could not proceed further in this direction, and that the people of Fakanjok had thought my only object was to sight from afar a golden prairie and a blue range beyond. The latter is known to the French as "Tem," from a hillock crowned with a huge red-trunked tree of that name.

Opposition was useless, so we turned back some twenty minutes to a junction, and took the south-eastern instead of the eastern line. Here the country was higher and drier, more hilly and gravelly, the aneroid showing some 900 feet (29·11); it would be exceptionally healthy in any but the rainy season. Before the afternoon had well set in, a camping ground had been chosen in the tall, thin forest, near the confluence of two dwarf streams, whose vitreous waters, flowing over fine sand and quartz pebbles, were no small recommendation. As the cooking proceeded, frowning brows relaxed, and huge fires put to flight ill temper and the sandfly. I had proposed lashing my hammock to one of the tree-stumps, which are here some ten feet tall, the people, who swing themselves for the purpose of felling, declare the upper wood to be softer than below. "Public opinion," however, overruled me, and made it fast to two old trunks. The night was a succession of violent tornadoes, and during one of the most outrageous the upper half of a "triste lignum," falling alongside of and grazing my hammock, awoke me with its crash.

Next morning, when the rain had somewhat abated, I set out, by a path whose makers were probably the ape and the squirrel-hunter, in the direction of a rise, which the people called Mbíká—The hill. After a total of some two miles and a half, we found a clearing upon the summit, but, although I climbed up a tree, the bush was dense enough to conceal most of the surroundings. According to the Fá*n*, the Nkomo rises on the seaward or western face of this Mbíká, whilst the Mbokwe, springing from its eastern counterslope, runs south-west of the Massif and joins the former. The one-tree hill known as "Tem" appeared a little to the north of west: to the north-east we could see a river-fork, but none knew its name.

Our return was enlivened by the inspection of an elephant-kraal, where a herd had been trapped, drugged, and shot during the last season. As the walls were very flimsy, I asked why the animals did not break loose; the answer was that the Ngá*n* (Mganga or Fetishman) ran a line of poison vine along its crest, and that the beasts, however wild, would not attempt to pass through it. The natives showed me the llana which they described, still lying on the poles of the broken corral. Mr. Preston, of the Gaboon Mission, who first noticed it, and Mr. Wilson, who gives an illustration of the scene (p. 363), declares that the creeper is drawn around the herd when browsing; that as long as the animals are unmolested they will not dash through the magic circle, and that the fence of uprights is constructed *outside* it. The same tale is told of all the wild elephant-hunters in the interior, the Báti the Okáná, the Yefá, and the Sensobá.

Arrived at Tippet-town, I gave my "dashes," chiefly brass and copper rods, bade an affectionate farewell, and then dropped down stream without further ceremony. I had been disappointed a second time *in re* gorilla, and nothing now remained but a retreat, which time rendered necessary. The down-stream voyage was an easy matter, and it need hardly be said far less unpleasant than the painful toil up. From the Sanjika village on the Gaboon, the "Tem" hill was seen bearing due east (Mag.) and the Mbíká 92°. Behind them were glimpses of blue highland, rising in lumpy and detached masses to the east; these are evidently sub-ranges of the western Ghats, the Sierra del Crystal, which native travellers described to me as a serrated broken line of rocky and barren acicular mountains; tall, gravelly, waterless, and lying about three days' journey beyond the screen of wooded hill. It is probably sheltered to some extent from the damp sea-breeze, and thus to the east there would be a "lee-land," dry, healthy and elevated, which, corresponding with Ugogo on the Zanzibar-Tanganyika line, would account for the light complexions of the people. Early on the morning of Thursday, April 17th, the "Eliza" was lying off Mr. R. B. N. Walker's factory, and I was again received with customary hospitality by Mr. Hogg.

These two short trips gave me a just measure of the comparative difficulties in travelling through Eastern and Western Africa, and to a certain extent accounted for the huge vacuum which disfigures the latter, a few miles behind the seaboard. The road to Unyamwezi, for instance, has been trodden for centuries; the people have become trained porters; they look forward annually to visiting the coast, and they are accustomed to the sight of strangers, Arabs and others. If war or blood-feud chance to close one line, the general interests of the interior open another. But in this section of Africa there is no way except from village to village, and a blood-feud may shut it for months. The people have not the habit of dealing with the foreigner, whom they look upon as a portent, a walking ghost, an ill-omened apparition. Porterage is in embryo, no scale of payment exists; and no dread of cutting off a communication profitable to both importer and exporter prevents the greedy barbarian plundering the stranger. Captain Speke and I were fortunate in being the first whites who seriously attempted the Lake Region; our only obstacles were the European merchants at Zanzibar; the murder of M. Maizan, although a bad example to the people, had been so punished as to render an immediate repetition of the outrage improbable. I say immediate, for, shortly after our return, the unfortunate Herr Roscher was killed at the Hisonguni village, near the Rufuma River, without apparent reason.[1]

But M. du Chaillu had a very different task, and as far as he went he did it well. His second expedition, in which an accidental death raised the country against him, was fortunately undertaken by a man in the prime of youth and strength; otherwise he must have succumbed to a nine hours' run, wounded withal. In East Africa when one of Lieutenant Cameron's "pagazis" happened to kill a native, the white man was mulcted only in half his cloth.

On the other hand, I see no reason why these untrodden lines should be pronounced impossible, as a writer in the "Pall Mall" has lately done, deterring the explorer from work which every day

---

[1] "Zanzibar City, Island, and Coast," vol. ii. chap. ii.

would cover new ground. The Gaboon is by no means a bad *point de départ*, whence the resolute traveller, with perseverance (*Anglicè* time), a knowledge of the coast language, and good luck might penetrate into the heart (proper) of Africa, and abolish the white blot which still affronts us. His main difficulty would be the heavy outlay; "impecuniosity" to him would represent the scurvy and potted cat of the old Arctic voyager. But if he can afford to travel regardless of delays and expense, and to place depots of cloth, beads, and other "country-money" at every hundred miles, Mpongwe-land would be one of the gateways to the unknown regions of the Dark Continent. Moreover, every year we hear some new account of travellers coming from the East. Unfortunately men with £5,000 to £20,000 a year do not "plant the lance in Africa," the old heroic days of the Spanish and Portuguese exploring hidalgos have yet to dawn anew. We must now look forward to subsidies from economical governments, and whilst the Germans and Italians, especially the former, are so liberally supported and adequately rewarded, Englishmen, as in the case of the gallant Lieutenant Cameron, run the risk of being repudiated, left penniless in the depths of Negroland.

CHAPTER XI.

MR., MRS., AND MASTER GORILLA.

HE reader will kindly bear in mind, when perusing my notes upon the gorilla, that, as in the the case of the Fá*n* cannibalism described by the young French traveller, my knowledge of the anthropoid is confined to the maritime region; moreover, that it is hearsay, fate having prevented my nearer acquaintance with the "ape of contention."

The discovery must be assigned to Admiral Hanno of Carthage, who, about B.C. 500, first in the historical period slew the Troglodytes, and carried home their spoils.

The next traveller who described the great Troglodytes of equatorial Africa was the well-known Andrew Battel, of Leigh, Essex (1589 to 1600); and his description deserves quoting. "Here (Mayombo) are two kinds of monsters common to these woods. The largest of them is called Pongo in their language, and the other Engeco" (in the older editions "Encêgo" evidently Nchígo, whilst Engeco may have given rise to our "Jocko"). "The Pongo is in all his proportions like a man, except the legs, which have no calves, but are of a gigantic size. Their faces, hands, and ears are without hair; their bodies are covered, but not very thick, with hair of a dunnish colour. *When they walk on the ground it is upright, with their hands on the nape of the neck.* They sleep in trees, and *make a covering over their heads to shelter them from the rain.* They eat no flesh, but feed on nuts and other fruits; they cannot speak, nor have they any understanding beyond instinct.

"When the people of the country travel through the woods, they make fires in the night, and in the morning, when they are gone, the Pongos will come and sit round it till it goes out, for they do not possess sagacity enough to lay more wood on. They go in bodies, and kill many negroes who travel in the woods. When elephants happen to come and feed where they are, they will fall on them, and so *beat them with their clubbed fists* (*sticks?*) that they are forced to run away roaring. The grown Pongos are never taken alive, owing to their strength, which is so great that ten men cannot hold one of them. The young Pongos hang upon their mother's belly, with their hands clasped about her. Many of the young ones are taken by means of shooting the mothers with poisoned arrows, and the young ones, hanging to their mothers, are easily taken."

I have italicized the passages which show that the traditions still preserved on the coast, about the Pongo and the Chimpanzee, date from old. Surely M. du Chaillu does grave injustice to this good old Briton, who was not a literary man, by declaring his stories to be mere travellers' tales, "untrue of any of the great apes of Africa." Battel had evidently not seen the animal, and with his negro informants he confounds the gorilla and the "bushman;" yet he possibly alludes to a species which has escaped M. du Chaillu and other modern observers.

Mr. W. Winwood Reade ("Savage Africa," chap. xix.) has done good service by reprinting the letter of a Bristol trader on the west coast of Africa, first published by Lord Monboddo ("Origin and Progress of Language," vol. i. p. 281, 1774 to 1792). Here we find distinct mention of three anthropoid apes. The first is the "Impungu" (or pongo?), which walks upright, and is from seven to nine feet high. The second is the "Itsena," evidently the Njína, Njí, Nguyla, or gorilla; and thirdly is the "Chimpenza," our Chimpanzee, a word corrupted from the Congoese Kampenzy, including the Nchígo, the Kulu-Kamba, and other Troglodytes. I have heard of this upright-walking Mpongo at Loango and other places on the west coast of Africa, where the Njína is familiarly spoken of, and it is not, methinks, impossible, that an ape even larger than the gorilla may yet be found.

James Barbot ("A Voyage to Congo River," Churchill, vol. v. p. 512,) tells us in 1700 that the "kingdom of *Angola*, or *Dongo*, produces many such extraordinary apes in the woods; they are called by the blacks *Quojas morrow*, and by the Indians *Orang-outang*, that is satyrs, or woodmen. . . . This creature seems to be the very satyr of the ancients, written of by *Pliny* and others, and is said to set upon women in the woods, and sometimes upon armed men." Amongst these animals he evidently includes the chimpanzee, as may be seen by his reference to the Royal Exchange, London.

In 1776 the philosophical Abbé Proyart, in his excellent "History of Loango," tells us (*vide* the chapter upon animals) that "there are in the forests baboons four feet high; the negroes affirm that, when they are hard pushed, they come down from the trees with sticks in their hands to defend themselves against those who are hunting them, and that very often they chase their pursuers. The missionaries never witnessed this singularity." According to the people, gorillas five or six feet tall have been seen as lately as 1840 at "Looboo Wood," a well-known spot which we shall presently sight, about three miles inland from the centre of Loango Bay.

And now the long intervals between travellers' accounts wax shorter. The well-known writer, Bowdich, before quoted, published, in 1819, his hearsay description of the "Ingena," garnished with the usual native tales. I had the honour of receiving an account of his discovery from his widow, the late Mrs. Lee, who was held the "mother of African travellers," and whose energy and intelligence endured to the last,—if memory serves me, she referred to some paper upon the subject, written by herself about 1825. Towards the end of 1846, the Rev. Mr. Wilson, founder of the Gaboon Mission, and proto-grammarian of its language, obtained two skulls, which were followed by skeletons, fragmentary and perfect. He sent No. 1, measuring, when alive, 5½ feet in height, and 4 feet across the shoulders, to the "Natural History Society" of Boston. He evidently has a right to boast that he was "the first to call the attention of *naturalists* to the 'Njena.'" His colleague, Dr. Thomas Savage, and Professor Jeffries Wyman called the new animal by the old name of gorilla, suffixing it to the "Troglodytes" which Geoffroy de Saint-Hilaire, reviving Linnæus, had proposed in 1812. In 1847, Dr. Savage published in the "Journal of Natural History" (Boston) the result of his careful inquiries about the

"Engé-ena" and the "Enche-eko." In 1852, this information was supplemented by Dr. Ford, also of the Gaboon Mission, with a "Paper on the Gorilla," published in the "Transactions of the Philadelphian Academy of Sciences."

M. du Chaillu first had the honour of slaying the gorilla in its native wilds. I saw his trophies in the United States in 1859; and the sensation which they subsequently created in London (1861-1862) is too recent to require notice. Unfortunately the specimens were mutilated and imperfect. Mr. R. B. N. Walker, agent of Messrs. Hatton and Cookson at the Gaboon River, was the first to send home a young specimen bodily, stowed away in spirits; two boiled skeletons of large grey animals, whose skins I saw at the factory, and rum-preserved brains, intestines, and other interesting parts, which had vainly been desired by naturalists. Mr. W. Winwood Reade spent five active months in the Gorilla country in 1862: Major Levison also visited the river, but their hunting was as unsuccessful as mine; whilst, in 1863, Major (now Colonel) De Ruvignes is reported to have been more fortunate. Since that time gorillas have been killed by the French chasseur.

The young Troglodyte has often been captured. The usual mode is to fell the tree, and during the confusion to throw a cloth over its head; the hands are then pinioned behind, and a forked stick is fastened under the chin to prevent the child biting. I should prefer, for trapping old as well as young, the way in which bears are caught by the North American backwoodsman,—a hollowed log, with some fruit, plantains for instance, floating in a *quant. suff.* of sugar, well sugared and narcotized.

Concerning the temper of these little captives, there are heroic differences of opinion. Mr. Ford records the "implacable desperation" of a juvenile which was brought to the Mission. It was taken very young, and kept four months, and many means were used to tame it; but it was so incorrigible, that it bit me an hour before it died." Yet, in face of this and other evidence, Mr. W. Winwood Reade, writing to the "Athenæum" (September 7, 1862), asserts that "the young gorilla in captivity is not savage." "Joe Gorilla," M. du Chaillu's brat, was notoriously fierce and unmanageable. The Rev. Mr. Walker, of Baraka, had a specimen, which he describes as a very tractable pupil; and my excellent friend Major Noeli y White, better known as "Governor White," of Corisco Island, brought to Fernando Po a baby Njína, which in its ways and manners much resembled an old woman. Mr. R. B. N. Walker became the happy godfather of two youngsters, who were different in disposition as Valentine and Orson. One, which measured 18 inches high, and died in 1861, was so savage and morose, that it was always kept chained; the other, "Seraphino," was of angelic nature, a general favourite at the Factory: it survives, in a photograph taken by the French Commandant of the Comptoir, as it sat after breakfast on godpapa's lap. At first it was confined, but it soon became so tame and playful, that the cage was required only at night. It never bit, unless when teased, and its only fault was not being able to avoid the temptation of eating what disagreed with it—in fact, it was sub-human in some points, and very human in others. All died in direct consequence of dysentery, which even a milk diet could not prevent. Perhaps the best way to send home so delicate an animal would be to keep it for a time in its native forest; to accustom it to boiled plantains, rice, and messes of grain; and to ship it during the fine season, having previously fitted up a cabin near the engine-room, where the mercury should never fall below 70° (Fahr.). In order to escape *nostalgia* and melancholy, which are sure to be fatal, the emigrant should be valeted by a faithful and attached native.

The habitat of the gorilla has been unduly limited to the left banks of the Gaboon and Fernão Vaz rivers, and to the lands lying between north latitude 2°, and south latitude 2°,—in fact, to the immediate vicinity of the equator.

The late Count Lavradio informed me that he had heard of it on the banks of the lower Congo River (south latitude 9°), and the "Soko," which Dr. Livingstone identifies with the Gorilla, extends to the Lualaba or Upper Congo, in the regions immediately west of the Tanganyika Lake. His friends have suggested that the "Soko" might have been a chimpanzee, but the old traveller was, methinks, far above making the mistake. The Yorubans at once recognize the picture; they call the anthropoid "Nákí;" and they declare that, when it seizes a man, it tears the fingers asunder. So M. du Chaillu (chapter vi.) mentions, in the Mpongwe report, that the Njína tears off the toe-nails and the finger-nails of his human captives. We should not believe so scandalous an assertion without detailed proof; it is hardly fair to make the innocent biped as needlessly cruel as man. It is well known to the natives of the Old Calabar River by the name of "Omon." In 1860, the brothers Jules and Ambroise Poncet travelled with Dr. Peney to Ab Kúka, the last of their stations near the head of the Luta Nzige (Albert Nyanza) Lake, and Dr. Peney "brought back the hand of the first gorilla which had been heard of" ("Ocean Highways," p. 482—February, 1874). The German Expedition (1873) reports Chicambo to be a gorilla country; that the anthropoid is found one day's journey from the Coast, and that the agent of that station has killed five with his own hand. Mr. Thompson of Sherbro ("Palm Land," chap. xiii.) says of the chimpanzee: "Some have been seen as tall as a man, from five to seven feet high, and very powerful." This is evidently the Njína, the only known anthropoid that attains tall human stature; and from the rest of the passage,[1] it is clear that he has confounded the chimpanzee with the Nchígo-mpolo.

The strip of gorilla-country visited by me was an elevated line of clayey and sandy soil, cut by sweet-water streams, and by mangrove-lined swamps, backed inland by thin forest. Here the comparative absence of matted undergrowth makes the landscape sub-European, at least, by the side of the foul tropical jungle; it is exceptionally rich in the wild fruits required by the huge anthropoid. The clearings also supply bananas, pine-apple leaves, and sugar-cane, and there is an abundance of honey, in which, like the Nchígo, the gorilla delights. The villages and the frequent plantations which it visits to plunder limit its reproduction near the sea, and make it exceedingly wary and keen of eye, if not of smell. Even when roosting by night, it is readily frightened by a footstep; and the crash caused by the mighty

---

[1] See chap. ii.

bound from branch to branch makes the traveller think that a tree has fallen.

The gorilla breeds about December, a cool and dry month : according to my bushmen, the period of gestation is between five and six months. The babe begins to walk some ten days after birth; "chops milk" for three months and, at the end of that time may reach eighteen inches in height. M. du Chaillu makes his child, "Joe Gorilla," 2 feet 6 inches when under the third year: assuming the average height of the adult male at 5 feet to 5 feet 6 inches, this measurement suggests that, according to the law of Flourens, the life would exceed thirty years. I saw two fragmentary skins, thoroughly "pepper and salt;" and the natives assured me that the gorilla turns silver-white with age.

It is still a disputed point whether the weight is supported by the knuckles of the forehand, like the chimpanzee, or whether the palm is the proper fulcrum. M. du Chaillu says ("First Expedition," chap. xx.), "the fingers are only lightly marked on the ground;" yet a few pages afterwards we are told, "The most usual mode of progression of the animal is on all-fours and resting on the knuckles." In the "Second Expedition" (chap. ii.) we read, "The tracks of the feet never showed the marks of toes, only the heels, and the track of the hands showed simply the impressions of the knuckles."

The attack of the gorilla is that of the apes and the monkeys generally. The big-bellied satyr advances to the assault as it travels, shuffling on all-fours; "rocking" not traversing; bristling the crest, chattering, mowing and displaying the fearful teeth and tusks. Like all the Simiads, this Troglodyte sways the body to and fro, and springs from side to side for the purpose of avoiding the weapon. At times Quasimodo raises himself slightly upon the dwarfed "asthenogenic," and almost deformed hind limbs, which look those of a child terminating the body of a Dan Lambert: the same action may be seen in its congeners great and small. The wild huntsmen almost cried with laughter when they saw the sketches in the "Gorilla Book,"[1] the mighty pugilist standing stiff and upright as the late Mr. Benjamin Caunt, "beating the breast with huge fists till it sounded like an immense bass drum;" and preparing to deal a buffet worthy of Friar Tuck. They asked me if I thought mortal man would ever attempt to face such a thing as that? With respect to drumming with both forehands upon the chest, some asserted that such is the brute's practice when calling Mrs. Gorilla, or during the excitement of a scuffle; but the accounts of the bushmen differ greatly on this point. In a hand-to-hand struggle it puts forth one of the

---

[1] First Edition, Illustration VI. (p. 71), and XLIII. (p. 297).

giant feet, sometimes the hinder, as "Joe Gorilla" was wont to do; and, having once got a hold with its prehensile toes, it bites and worries like any other ape, baboon, or monkey. From this grapple doubtless arose the old native legend about the gorilla drawing travellers up trees and "quietly choking them." It can have little vitality, as it is easily killed with a bit of stone propelled out of a trade musket by the vilest gunpowder, and the timid bushmen, when failing to shoot it unawares, do not fear to attack it openly. As a rule, the larger the Simiad, the less sprightly it becomes; and those most approaching man are usually the tamest and the most melancholy—perhaps, their spirits are permanently affected by their narrow escape. The elderly male (for anthropoids, like anthropoi, wax fierce and surly with increasing years) will fight, but only from fear, when suddenly startled, or with rage when slightly wounded. Moreover, there must be rogue-gorillas, like rogue-elephants, lions, hippopotami, rhinoceros, and even stags, *vieux grognards*, who, expelled house and home, and debarred by the promising young scions from the softening influence of feminine society, become, in their enforced widowerhood, the crustiest of old bachelors. At certain seasons they may charge in defence of the wife and family, but the practice is exceptional. Mr. Wilson saw a man who had lost the calf of his leg in an encounter, and one

Etia, a huntsman whose left hand had been severely crippled, informed Mr. W. Winwood Reade, that "the gorilla seized his wrist with his hind foot, and dragged his hand into his mouth, as he would have done a bunch of plantains." No one, however, could give me an authentic instance of manslaughter by our big brother.

The modifications with which we must read the picturesque pages of the "Gorilla Book" are chiefly the following. The Gorilla is a poor devil ape, not a "hellish dream-creature, half man, half beast." He is not king of the African forest; he fears the Njego or leopard and, as lions will not live in these wet, wooded, and gameless lands, he can hardly have expelled King Leo. He does not choose the "darkest, gloomiest forests," but prefers the thin woods, where he finds wild fruits for himself and family. His tremendous roar does not shake the jungle: it is a hollow apish cry, a loudish huhh! huhh! huhh! explosive like the puff of a steam-engine, which, in rage becomes a sharp and snappish bark—any hunter can imitate it. Doubtless, in some exceptional cases, when an aged mixture of Lablache and Dan Lambert delivers his *voce di petto*, the voice may be heard for some distance in the still African shades, but it will hardly compare with the howling monkeys of the Brazil, which make the forest hideous. The eye is not a "light grey" but the brown common to all the tribe. The Gorilla cannot stand straight upon his rear quarter when attacking or otherwise engaged without holding on to a trunk : he does not "run on his hind legs ;" he is essentially a tree ape, as every stuffed specimen will prove. He never gives a tremendous blow with his immense open paw ; doubtless, a native legend found in Battel and Bowdich ; nor does he attack with the arms. However old and male he may be, he runs away with peculiar alacrity : though powerfully weaponed with tigerish teeth, with "bunches of muscular fibre," and with the limbs of Goliah, the gorilla, on the seaboard at least, is essentially a coward ; nor can we be surprised at his want of pluck, considering the troubles and circumstances under which he spends his harassed days. Finally, whilst a hen will defend her chicks, Mrs. Gorilla will fly, leaving son or daughter in the hunter's hands.

CHAPTER XII.

CORISCO—"HOME" TO FERNANDO PO.

N April 22nd, after some five weeks in the Gaboon River, I found myself once more in her Majesty's steam-ship "Griffon," which had returned from the south coast, bound for Corísco (Gorilla Island?) and Fernando Po. It was "going-away day," when proverbially the world looks prettier than usual, and we enjoyed the suggestive view of the beaded line which, seen from the sea, represents the Sierra del Crystal. The distance from Le Plateau to the Isle of Lightning was only thirty-five miles, from the nearest continent ten, and before the evening tornado broke from the south-east, here the normal direction, we were lying in the roads about two miles from the landing-place. The anchorage is known by bringing Mbánya (Little Corisco), the smaller and southern outlier in a line between Laval Islet and the main island.

The frequent coruscations gave a name to

Corisco, which the natives know as Mange: it was called, says Barbot, "'Ilha do Corisco,' from the Portuguese, because of the violent horrid lightnings, and claps of thunder, the first discoverers there saw and heard there at the time of their discovery." There is still something to be done in investigating the cause of these electrical discharges. Why should lofty Fernando Po and low-lying Corisco suffer so much, when Zanzibar Island, similarly situated, suffers so rarely? Again, why is Damascus generally free from thunder-storms when Brazilian Sâo Paul, whose site is of the same altitude and otherwise so like, can hardly keep the lightning out of doors? The immunity of Zanzibar Island can hardly be explained by the popular theory; neither it nor Fernando Po, which suffers greatly from thunder-storms, lies near the embouchure of a great river; where salt and fresh water may disturb electrical equilibrium. I shall say more upon this point when in the Congo Regions (chap. xii.).

The position of Great Corisco (north latitude 0° 55′ 0″) is at the mouth of a well-wooded bay, which Barbot (iv. 9) calls Bay of Angra, *i.e.* Bight of Bight. He terms the southern or Munda stream Rio de Angrta, or Angex, whilst the equally important Muni (Danger) becomes only "a little river" without name. The modern charts prefer Corisco Bay. It measures some forty miles from north to south by half that depth, and its position causes the rains, which are synchronous with those of the Gaboon, to be much more copious and continuous. They last nine months out of twelve, and in March, 1862, the fall was 25 inches, the heaviest remembered:

TADI NZAZHI, THE "LIGHTNING ROCK."

it had filled the little island valleys, and made the paths lines of canal.

Next morning we were visited by the Rev. Mr. Mackey, the senior of the eight white men who inhabit this piece of land—a proper site for Robinson Crusoe—where, as the Yankee said of Great Britain, you can hardly stretch yourself without fear of falling overboard. He kindly undertook to be our guide over the interior, and we landed on the hard sand of the open western beach: here at times a tremendous surf must roll in. We struck into the bush, and bent towards the south-west of the islet, where stands the monarch of cliffs, 80 feet high. The maximum length is three miles by about the same breadth, and the circumference, including the indentations, may be fifteen. The surface is rolling composed of humus and clay, corallines and shelly conglomerates based on tertiary limestone and perhaps sandstone; dwarf clearings alternate with tracts of bush grass, and with a bushy second growth, lacking large trees. The only important wild productions pointed out to us were cardamoms, the oil palm (*Elais Guineensis*), and an unknown species of butter-nut. The centre of the island was a mass of perennial pools, fed, they say, by springs as well as rains, one puddle, adorned with water lilies and full of dwarf leeches which relish man's life, extended about a hundred yards long. In fact, the general semblance of Corisco was that of a filled up "atoll," a circular reef still growing to a habitable land. Here only could I find on the west coast of Africa a trace of the features which distinguished the Gorilla island of 2,300 years ago.

At South Bay we came upon a grassy clearing larger than usual, near a bright stream; its pottery and charred wood showed the site of the Spanish barracoon destroyed by the British in 1840. During the last seven years the "patriarchal institution" has become extinct, and the old slavers who have at times touched at the island, have left it empty-handed. Corisco had long been celebrated for cam-wood, a hard and ponderous growth, yielding a better red than Brazil or Braziletto, alias Brazilete (*Brasilettia*, De Cand.) one of the *Eucæsalpinieæ*, a congener of *C. Echinata*, which produces the Brazil-wood or Pernambuco-wood of commerce. In 1679, the Hollander Governor-General of Minas sent some forty whites to cultivate "Indian wheat and other sort of corn and plants of Guinea." The design was to supply the Dutch West Indian Company's ships with grain and vegetables, especially bananas, which grow admirably; I heard that there are fifteen varieties upon this dot of dry land. Thus the crews would not waste time and money at Cape Lopez and the Portuguese islands. The Dutch colonists began by setting up a factory in a turf redoubt, armed with iron guns, "the better to secure themselves from any surprise or assault of the few natives, who are a sort of wild and mischievous blacks." The plantation was successful, but the bad climate and noxious gases from the newly turned ground, combined with over-exertion, soon killed some seventeen out of the forty; and the remainder, who also suffered from malignant distempers, razed their buildings and returned to the Gold Coast. When the Crown of Spain once more took possession of Fernando Po, it appointed a Governor for Corisco, but no establishment was maintained there. To its credit be it said, there was not much interference with the Protestant mission; public preaching was forbidden *pro formâ* in 1860, but no notice was taken of "passive resistance."

The native villages, exactly resembling those of the Gaboon, are all built near the strip of fine white sand which forms the shore, and upon the sweet water channels which cut deep into the limestones. They are infested with rats, against whose depredations the mango trees must be protected with tin ruffs; yet there are six kinds of *reptilia* upon the island, including the common black snake and cobras, from six to seven feet long: these animals, aided by the dogs, which also persecute the iguanas, have prevented rabbits breeding. In Barbot's time (1700) there were only thirty or forty inhabitants, who held the north-eastern point about a league from the wooding and watering places. "That handful of blacks has much ado to live healthy, the air being very intemperate and unwholesome; they are governed by a chief, who is lord of the island, and they all live very poorly, but have plenty enough of cucumbers, which grow there in perfection, and many sorts of fowl." In 1856 the Rev. Mr. Wilson reckons them at less than 2,000, and in 1862 I was told that there were about 1,100, of whom 600 were Bengas. In look, dress, and ornaments they resemble the Mpongwe, but some of them have adopted the Kru stripe, holding a blue nose to be a sign of freedom. They consider themselves superior to the "Pongos," and they have exchanged their former fighting reputation for that of peaceful traders to the mainland and to the rivers Muni and Mundah. They live well, eating flesh or fish once a day, not on Sundays only, the ambition of Henri Quatre: at times they trap fine green turtle in seines, but they do not turn these "delicate monsters."

Mr. Wilson numbered the whole Benga tribe at 8,000, but Mr. Mackey reduced the figure to half. Besides Corisco they inhabit the two capes at the north and south of the bay. The language is used by other tribes holding the coast northward for a hundred miles or more, and probably by the inner people extending in a northerly direction from Corisco Bay: the same, with certain modifications, is also spoken at São Bento, Batanga, and perhaps as far north as the Camarones River. On the other hand, the tribes occupying the eastern margin of Corisco Bay, such as the Mbiko, Dibwe, and Belengi, cannot understand one another, and the tongues of the southward regions differ even more from the Benga. Yet all evidently belong to the great South African family.

Mr. Mackey, who explored Corisco Island in 1849, assures us that scarcely any of the older inhabitants were born there; they came from the continent north or north-east of the bay, gradually forcing their way down. The characteristic difference of the Benga, the Bákele, and the Mpongwe dialects is as follows: "The Mpongwes have a great partiality for the use of the passive voice, and avoid the active when the passive can be used. The Bákele verb delights in the active voice, and will avoid the passive even by a considerable circumlocution. The Benga takes an intermediate position in this respect, and uses the active and passive very much as we do in English."

The Corisco branch of the Presbyterian Board of Foreign Missions was established by the Rev. James S. Mackey in 1850. It made as much progress as could be expected, and in 1862 it numbered 110 scholars and 65 communicants; the total of those baptized was 80, and 15 had been suspended. The members applied themselves, as the list of their publications shows, with peculiar ardour to the language, and they did not neglect natural history and short explorations of the adjoining interior. They had sent home specimens of the six *reptilia*, the six snails and land shells, the seventy-five sea shells, and the 110 fishes, all known by name, which they collected upon the island and in the bay. It is to be presumed that careful dredging will bring to light many more: the pools are said to produce a small black fish, local as the *Proteus anguineus* of the Styrian caves, to mention no other.

I was curious to hear from Mr. Mackey some details about the Muni River, where he travelled in company with M. du Chaillu. It still keeps the troublous reputation for petty wars which made the old traders dignify it with the name of "Danger." The nearest Falls are about thirty miles from Olobe Island, and the most distant may be sixty-five. Of course we had a laugh over the famous Omamba or Anaconda, whose breath can be felt against the face before it is seen.

Late in April 24th I returned the books kindly lent to me from the mission library, shook hands with my kind and hospitable entertainers at the mission house, mentally wishing them speedy deliverance from Corisco, and embarked on board the "Griffon." We quickly covered the "great water desert" of 160 miles between the Gorilla Island and Fernando Po, and at noon on the next day I found myself once more "at home."

PRINTED BY WHITTINGHAM AND WILKINS,
TOOKS COURT, CHANCERY LANE.

For EU product safety concerns, contact us at Calle de José Abascal, 56–1°, 28003 Madrid, Spain or eugpsr@cambridge.org.

www.ingramcontent.com/pod-product-compliance
Ingram Content Group UK Ltd.
Pitfield, Milton Keynes, MK11 3LW, UK
UKHW010346140625
459647UK00010B/871